Contents

Aileen Friedl (signature)

Teaching Adults
An Active Learning Approach

Elizabeth Jones
Pacific Oaks College

A 1985–1986 NAEYC
Comprehensive Membership Benefit

National Association for
the Education of Young Children
Washington, D.C.

Book design: Cynthia Faber

Library of Congress Catalog Card Number: 85-63557
ISBN Catalog Number: 0-912674-96-2

NAEYC #205

Printed in the United States of America

Preface

This is my third try at writing this book. NAEYC turned the first version down flat, and I didn't even bother to send the second. The previous versions were much broader than this one; full of generalizations about my experiences with adults as learners. I had forgotten—again—what I had previously discovered repeatedly: To teach and to write, I need to tell stories. In the middle of my revision process, Robert Coles gave a speech at Pacific Oaks, and he said the same thing: Don't generalize, tell stories.

Learning to do scholarly writing in order to survive in higher education, one is inclined to forget how to tell stories. Sober comments on data in tables are much more respectable. But what all of us really *know*, what informs our behavior as teachers or parents or in whatever we do, we know from the vivid, unforgettable details of our experience—experience that fits into the patterns we keep building to make sense of our world. And experience can be shared vicariously; we also remember others' stories, written or told.

This book is a story. I have experienced most of it, imagined some of it, creating a course that *could* have happened this way. I have chosen to write about teaching child development because, as everyone knows, that's the important course, the one that really matters. College teachers often play around with the design of their other courses—curriculum, child/family and community, even administration—but child development is *theory*, and therefore it must be *taught.* No fooling around with this one.

I agree: Child development is the important course. I care about theory, and I want students to learn it. But I don't think many students learn it very well by listening to lectures, reading the textbook, or memorizing, even though some of them can parrot it back on the exam. Theory is learned through action and interaction, through relating it to one's own experience. Cognitive learning requires attention to affective learning: Anxiety must be recognized, trust built, and interpersonal skills and self-esteem fostered. Child development is a highly affect-laden subject, and if students are to learn it, they need to come to terms with their feelings about it.

The problem, of course, is that when you ask college students to *do* things in a course—play with materials, play with each other, talk about their own childhoods, be quiet and go back in their memories—it doesn't feel serious. We have been learning ever since we were in kindergarten that only papers and books and records are serious. If your kindergarten was like mine, your teacher discouraged you from bringing toys to show-and-tell, or kittens, or your baby brother, or your grandpa. You were only supposed to bring educational things. What's educational? That is a difficult distinction for a 5-year-old. And the teacher wasn't altogether clear. She really did get enthusiastic about Jody's bird's nest, but we soon learned that it was always safe to bring books and records, and so those, we figured, must be the most educational things. And it was generally a good idea to play it safe in kindergarten. Even if you had a nice teacher, you didn't always know how she would react. Best to please her. Also it was clear that she thought papers—dittos and dittos and dittos—and books were really imporant. Sand and games were only for recess, and while you did get to build with blocks, maybe, she talked a lot about shapes and colors and airports and garages while you were doing that. She liked letters and numbers best.

Every year, kindergartens seem to get clearer on this point. In the kindergarten my children went to there aren't any blocks now. And there is hardly anything to play with in school once you are past kindergarten. So it is no wonder that both college students and their teachers are very clear that you do not learn about child development by playing—only through the experts' words in books and papers and lectures.

I don't agree. But then I think that preschools, where teachers still believe that children learn through play, are the best thing in American education. Further, I believe that we don't stop learning through play just because we're grown up. Learning through play includes playing with the possibilities, being flexible, staying loose when things go wrong, being curious, thinking creatively, and problem solving.

Finally, I believe people who are going to become teachers of young children should be taught in the same way I hope they will teach. Katz (1977) has called this the Principle of Congruity—that adults be treated according to the developmental principles they must follow in working with young children. Good teachers are playful; they don't take themselves too seriously.

Like any story, this one has implications for other experiences too. It may be useful to people teaching other college courses, in teacher education, and perhaps in other fields as well. And it is relevant not only to college teaching, but to the varied settings—conferences, parent groups, adult education, staff development, in-service workshops—where adults come together to learn about children and themselves.

This story happened at Pacific Oaks College, which is an unusual place as far as colleges go. It's small, with some 300 upper-division and graduate students, most of them beyond college age. It's independent and flexible, allowing teachers of both adults and children an unusual degree of autonomy. Faculty and administration share the conviction that autonomy in decision making and problem solving contributes both to knowledge and to self-esteem, and thus, to competence in one's works and one's life. Much of what we do with adults at Pacific Oaks is based on our understanding of child development, extended into adulthood. We were a children's school before we became a college, and we see a school for children as peopled with learners working together on many different levels. Likewise the college. If I am a learner when I teach children, I must remain a learner when I teach adults. I must respect their ability to make good choices for themselves just as I respect children's.

People who are going to be teachers of young children should be taught in the same way they will teach.

Programs for young children at Pacific Oaks are based on an open-classroom model, in which children choose the majority of their own activities.

> Adults are responsible for structuring an environment full of developmentally appropriate choices, helping children choose among the possibilities, and enriching their experience by joining in it and building on it. The notion of "teacher-proof" curricula, rationally designed by specialists to insure excellence of instruction regardless of the teacher's skill, has no place in such a classroom. Standardized plans made by someone outside a setting as complex as a day-to-day class of children cannot possibly be appropriate to the unique events which keep happening in that class. Good curriculum emerges out of those unique events. . . .
>
> We see teaching as an art, not a predictable science. It is learned by doing and by continual question-asking and reflection. Learners are individuals, and their interests and unique characteristics need to be taken seriously. Teaching and learning involve a relationship between persons who need to work continually at understanding each other. These are the assumptions which underlie the open classroom at Pacific Oaks.
>
> (Jones, 1978, p.1)

As a college teacher at Pacific Oaks, I actively participate in the faculty process which determines course offerings, and I have a reasonable opportunity to choose what, when, where, and how I teach. Risk-taking is valued; this is a good place to try out new ideas. The place you teach may be quite different. But that does not, in my view, mean that the approach developed at Pacific Oaks, and described here, is altogether inapplicable in your setting. If that's a particular concern for you, you might like to begin this book with Chapter 18, the Postscript, in which I describe strategies that I and others have used in teaching adults in other settings. Read that, and then decide if you want to read the rest.

Thirty-five students of widely varied age and experience have enrolled in my child development class. I sit and watch them as they straggle into the room. Several of them I already know, and that relieves some of my anxiety about starting a new class. I say "Hi, it's good to see you." They smile back, though Joan's smile is shaky. Another year, another new class with which to cope. She's not very secure, as a person or as a student.

In the middle of the doorway sits a chair with a sign, Take One and Begin, taped to its back, and a pile of directions, Getting Acquainted (Appendix), on the seat. Some students notice and pick up a copy of the directions. Others push on by and sit down.

I have structured this beginning to enable me to observe and interact with individual students, just as I would do with young children. In most college classes the opposite is true; the instructor is the only actor and the students get to do all the observing. That doesn't serve my purpose, which is to get to know each student in the context of this child development course.

The chairs are arranged in a double circle, and I've put several cushions on the floor in the middle. On a table lies paper, several felt pens, and a dish of pins. A dozen students have clustered around the table and are writing children's names on papers. The rest are sitting in chairs; one is knitting, three are reading, a couple are talking, and the rest appear to be waiting for class to begin. I pick up several Getting Acquainteds and approach them. "Did you get one of these?" Some did but haven't looked at it. I suggest they read #1 and begin. I hand a sheet to each person who didn't get one and repeat my suggestion. "You really do have to get up and walk around," I assure them.

One student chuckles at me. "This is different." Another looks confused and unhappy. I smile at her, I hope reassuringly. Students have such fixed notions of how a college class is supposed to be. Some will be delighted to discover this one is different; others won't like that at

1

Getting Started

Lively motion is more exciting, and even more educational, than sitting quietly.

Many students are interested in teaching. Therefore I'm particularly interested in demystifying teaching for them, at the college level as well as with young children.

Subjects & Predicates

all. They have a whole repertoire of survival behaviors: lie low, take notes, sit in an inconspicuous place so you won't get called on, study hard for the exam. They've made it this far. They've passed. They don't want the boat rocked.

And here I am, a boat rocker, needing to help them understand that this boat is really an unsinkable Boston whaler, and that lively motion is more exciting, and even more educational, than sitting quietly—afraid of making waves, afraid of getting seasick and being conspicuous. The good sailors are OK, they always have been; they can speak up and be noticed because they're used to winning. Amy's one of those, and Sarah, and Bob, too. But the Joans are in the majority in many classes; they've had too many messages from teachers: You're not good enough. That's what a C tells students. That's how some students read a B, too.

Joan has found a partner; good for her. Or maybe her partner took the initiative. Their conversation is getting more animated as they begin to relax with each other. "I couldn't stand that child's whining!" I overhear as I walk past them. At least five students haven't found a partner yet. I ask them if they need help, pair a couple of them, and end up as a partner myself to even it all out. I ask my partner about Jason, age 4, about whom she has written *funny* and *loud*. And I respond to her questions about Megan, age 8, gentle and undependable. I try to keep track of what's happening in the room while paying attention to my partner: a useful skill, dual-focusing. I learned it as a preschool teacher.

A student comes in late, and I excuse myself to help her get started. I ask my partner if she would mind having a new partner, helping Marilyn join in. I don't really give her a choice, but she doesn't seem to mind. She's already done it with me; she knows how now. I go back to observing.

By this time people are at different places on the list of directions. I count six foursomes, while some pairs are still going strong. A few people are writing; have they really gotten to #7, or are they skipping around? I don't mind if they skip around; my sequence doesn't have to be theirs. I want these prospective teachers to learn, from their own experience, that individual learners' rhythms are different, that this is a resource-full environment in which information is available for the looking, and that it isn't necessary to wait for a teacher to tell you things or even, to get started, to know who the teacher is. Getting Acquainted is designed as a closed-to-open task (Jones, 1973). It begins with closed directions: Do this, and this. But what students say and whom they say it to are open, and no one checks to see if they did it right. Closed-to-open is a very useful getting-started sequence for adults and other people who have learned to do what they're told in school. (It isn't so useful for preschoolers, who are better at taking initiative.)

As in preschool, I begin by observing. But as in preschool, the real beginning happens earlier, as I plan care-

Closed-to-open is a very useful getting-started sequence for people who have learned to do what they're told in school.

3

fully and set up the environment so students will have things to do. In setting up the environment, I have developed a whole set of criteria to match my educational goals; and because the outcome is so unfamiliar to most students, I try throughout the course to explain to them what I'm trying to do and why. Many of my students are interested in teaching as a career. Therefore I'm particularly interested in demystifying teaching for them, at the college level as well as with young children. I am a teacher, this is what I'm trying to do, this is how I'm going about it. I want you to pay attention to what I'm doing and how it works for you as a learner and for those other learners. I will ask you for continuing feedback, so we can plan together.

My notes for the first session of this 3-hour class estimate time blocks as follows:

1:00–2:15   Getting acquainted
2:15–2:45   Class meeting
2:45–3:45   Small groups: value choices
3:45–4:00   Discussion of value choices

I'm running a little behind, as usual, when I ask everyone to come together at 2:20. I explain briefly that this class will be more active than some they have had, because I really want them to learn child development theory, and I believe theory is understood only through experience. *What is it like to be a child?* is our basic question. I'll ask you to keep reflecting on experiences with children:

those you have already had
memories of your own childhood
the childhoods of other people in this group, remembered and shared
observations you make of children during the semester
other people's observations of children, including those in books.
In class we will share these experiences and participate

4

in some activities which may add to our understanding of what it's like to be a child. We'll talk about concepts which are useful in generalizing about child development and helping us to understand patterns in child behavior and growth. When I say *we*, I mean it. I'm learning about child development too, and I will be learning from you, because you have experiences that I haven't had.

As Things To Do (Appendix) indicates, I expect you to read, write, observe, and participate in class activities, because I think these are useful ways to learn. But I expect you to make choices concerning what to read or where to observe, for example, because each of you is different. It's your responsibility to make this class work for you and to complain when it isn't.

Questions?

There are several. There will be more later, I know from experience.

I ask them to look at Child Development: Some Basic Assumptions (Appendix) which they picked up during the get-acquainted process. I read through it.

Theories, I explain, look at regularities in development; they generalize about some of the ways in which children are alike. We will balance this by continuing to look at individual and cultural differences: How was your childhood different from that of the person sitting next to you, and why? How far can you move out of your own ego and ethnocentrism—*my* way is the right way—this semester? We'll work at it, me too. Here's a beginning.

We're going to form small groups by numbering off, to distribute everyone more or less randomly. Number from 1 to 7 and then start over. *Remember your number.* One! I point at the woman on my left, who looks startled but repeats "One." "Two" on her left, and around we go. One comes after seven, remember?

All right, will all the sevens collect in this corner? Sixes there, fives there . . . I check to make sure they're sorting themselves out. There should be five in each group. Now, sit together in a circle and find out when each person's

We generate our own curriculum.

birthday is. I'll come around to each group with task instructions.

I do, handing out Before Birth (Appendix).

Group 6 isn't sitting in a circle; they're stretched out in a line. I point out that a circle is round, and they need to be one. They laugh and shuffle chairs. One looks annoyed; she didn't want to move. I don't give her that choice.

Why all this tight, detailed structuring? Again, it's closed-to-open structure. This is the first day of class; it's hard to form spontaneous groups, and I've already asked them to do that twice. The point of this task is to experience diversity, so I don't want friends sitting together. I don't want them to spend time figuring out how to organize the task or whose turn it is. I want them to be able to hear each other, even with all these small groups talking simultaneously; that requires tight circles. I plan for the outcomes I want in activities like these, and structure accordingly.

When we come back together, I ask whether any groups reached consensus on any of the dilemmas. Not many, only Groups 2 and 3, which agreed that Terry should have an abortion. Group 3 also agreed on abortion for Jane and Janet. I don't prolong this discussion; they've already had it in their small groups, and it's time to go.

Who are these students? What do they already know about childhood? They have all been children. Some of them are parents. Most of them have worked with children as baby sitters, teacher assistants, caregivers, teachers, or camp counselors. What are their questions and concerns? And *they* is not a whole, it's a collection of individuals, each with different questions. I need to tune in to those questions, so I need a structure that will make that possible. They need to learn from each other's experience, and the structure needs to make that possible too. We will generate our own curriculum.

Overall, I feel pretty good about this first session; there was lots of interaction. Later, though, when I start reading folders, I realize that my plan gave me less feedback than I wanted. One of the things that still happens to me after more than 20 years of college teaching is that I keep forgetting what I know. I know it's important for students to learn each other's names, in order to make this structure work well; yet I forgot to ask people to make name tags. (I *always* ask people to make name tags.) Not only students, but I, had no handy way of starting to learn names at the first session, and that's usually one of the things I start doing immediately, while I'm observing. Further, in asking for written feedback I didn't ask the questions I usually ask: What was the best thing that happened for you in today's class? What bored or frustrated or bothered you? Feedback relieves my anxiety, even if some of it is negative; it puts me in touch with individuals, and I can start doing something about teaching to their needs.

The written response to the questions I did ask was pretty impersonal. I should have known it would be; people who don't know the teacher will try to give right answers, if the questions let them. I wanted to make it clear to people that they already know something about what we're going to study, and that the curriculum in this class will be responsive to their interests. Maybe it had that effect. But it didn't tell me much about them as individuals, as it turned out. In most classes I do a better job of making personal contact with students from the beginning, getting a sense of who they are and how they're feeling. That turned out to be a delayed process in this class.

This class meets weekly for 3 hours. I like that much better than shorter, more frequent classes; we have more time to get a variety of activities going. And it gives me time to read and respond to the writing in students' folders between every class.

In any class, it is important to begin by (1) defining the parameters of the setting (these are the things you can or cannot do here) and (2) establishing trust in the teacher

2

From Anxiety Toward Trust

(I am a competent teacher, I know what I'm doing, you can count on me). As long as either of these things remains unclear, students of any age will keep testing, questioning, and displaying anxiety. The clearer I can be about my expectations at the beginning of a class, the more likely students are to feel secure and trust me, themselves, and each other.

When students arrive at the second class meeting, there is a name tag for each of them pinned to the bulletin board, with a sign: Find Your Name Tag. Wear It. Learn at Least Five People's Names Before the End of Class Today.

It would have been simpler to have people make their own name tags. I made them because I wanted to play a classification game with them. I was glad I had when I read later in Joanne's folder:

> I was feeling uncertain after that first class. I think we all have the need of acceptance and some structure. I felt more acceptance tonight when there was a name tag on the board with my name on it. I judged someone was expecting me. To me a personal greeting by someone who has called us together helps to assure me I am in the right place. (Even a class list offers some security.)

Classification games of all sorts help people to make connections, to find people who are like them in some way, to engage in problem solving. Piaget emphasizes classification as critical to the development of cognition, and preschool teachers spend a lot of time encouraging children to classify things in their environment. I began this game with some of the information I already had about the class members: their addresses, and whether or not they were new to the college this semester. I coded each name tag with different colored gummed dots:

The clearer I can be about my expectations at the beginning, the more likely students are to feel secure and trust me, themselves, and each other.

Lives on each side of town	red
Lives on west side of town	blue
New student	light green
Old student	dark green
Male	orange
Female	purple

The gender code is easy for people to guess. The others are more difficult, requiring lots of question-asking, but they give people information which might be useful in making connections with each other. And I have a lot more dots up my sleeve, which I roam around adding to people's name tags as I look at them:

Wearing glasses	dark blue
Wearing sandals	pink
Wearing brown	brown
Wearing a skirt	black
Dark-haired	white

I keep (out of sight) my code list so I won't forget. The mere act of sticking dots on people makes the teacher a different sort of person—unwelcomely different, no doubt, to some, but a new element to be reckoned with. What *do* teachers do? Some teachers of young children think they are only teaching during a lesson. I like to keep complicating their definition of what teaching is; so I model a variety of behaviors for them.

To complicate their definition of what teaching is, I model a variety of behaviors.

The instructions for this game are "Figure out what the dots mean. You'll have to move around and talk to people." I allow a short time for this, then go on with some other activities, and then part way through the session ask the group what they figured out.

Silly games. I didn't use to play games in my classes at all, except my preschool classes. How could I ask adults to do things like that? I learned gradually, though, as I watched some of my students leading games in my classes and realized the positive impact of laughter, touch, and movement on people's capacity to relax and learn.

9

I have found that games build group cohesion. They help people get acquainted, encourage trust, practice communication, experience relaxation and/or mobility, and enjoy laughter. The authors of *Playfair* (Weinstein & Goodman, 1980) confirm my experience when they explain that games can be introduced into work places or classrooms

> as exercises to promote relaxation, as energizers, or as ways for people to make contact with each other on the feeling/sharing/frolicking level. . . . In our teaching and lecturing experience it has been demonstrated over and over that allowing our listeners repeated breaks from the "content" of a session (during which they play one of the *Playfair* games) allows them to participate in the content learning with renewed attention and energy. (pp. 124–125)

Writing as preparation for a discussion helps people focus.

That's been my experience too. In some classes I forget, and then I wonder why the group doesn't come together. In some classes a student takes the initiative. Last summer Julie, a movement specialist, asked if she could lead regular movement activities for the group. I wondered a little if the other students would see movement as relevant to the class content. Their comments made it clear that they understood the relationship between physical action and intellectual learning.

Back to this class. Last week, to begin, we talked about children we've known. That's a safer beginning than talking about our own childhoods, which we're going to do this week. After some milling about, I ask people to sit down and write about a childhood passion: What, at some point in your childhood, did you care very deeply about? What sort of acknowledgement did you get from adults?

Writing as preparation for a discussion, I have found, helps people focus. Many people have trouble thinking on their feet if they are suddenly asked to contribute an experience in front of the whole group. If they write first, and the quality of the writing itself is of no concern, they have a private space for remembering. Guided imagery

Stephanie Feeney

Games build group cohesion. They help people get acquainted, encourage trust, practice communication, experience relaxation and/or mobility, and enjoy laughter.

serves the same purpose—shut your eyes, go back in your memory—and I often use it. But at this session I have asked people to write, partly because I want them to get writing into their folders so I can get to know individuals quickly.

Ten minutes for writing, stretching into 15. Now, bring your chairs into a circle. We're going to talk about it.

A class of 35 is too large to do much sharing in the whole group. The size of the group frightens some stu-

11

dents—talking in front of all those people. The amount of time it takes to go around and have everyone share an experience is far too long; it risks becoming boring. On this occasion I'm risking it as part of the get-acquainted process. I want people to have a sense of who all those other people are. I'm counting on the diversity in a group this large to give us a wide range of examples. I'm also willing to take as much time as needed, even spilling over into next week. In other words, I have decided that childhood passions are a very important lead-in to a basic developmental principle: that motivation comes from within, and is idiosyncratic; and that reinforcing a child's own wishes and desires, whenever possible, helps that child continue to be a caring, motivated person.

We'll go around the circle. Tell us, when it's your turn, what you cared deeply about and what happened. If you want to pass, because this isn't something you want to share in the group, that's OK.

I begin, to model, to make it clear that I am a member of this group, not only its leader, and to avoid putting someone else on the spot.

> I cared passionately about the High Sierra, to which we went each summer on pack trips. I loved its beauty and wildness and the fact that there was nobody there but us. My parents, who took me in the first place because *they* cared passionately about wilderness, were delighted at my delight. Outcomes, for me: I still care more about mountains than any other terrain. When I lived in the Midwest I missed them rather desperately. I sit in window seats in airplanes and go slightly crazy every time another Cascade comes into view. We took our kids camping and they have all grown up to be environmentalists, with a clear sense of our obligations to Planet Earth.

Risk. What if students decide that my example is the right sort and hastily revise theirs to fit? Fortunately the student to my right has an altogether different passion, though she begins by apologizing for it and I assure her that it's fine.

> I wanted a Barbie doll, desperately. My mother thought they were vulgar and refused to buy me one. All my friends had them. I cried and pleaded and I think my daddy would have given in, but he didn't want to make my mother mad. I never got one. I haven't quite forgiven my mother.
>
> Would you get your child a Barbie doll? I ask.
>
> Oh, yes! I already did, and she's only four and I don't think she cares very much about it, but *I* needed it. Of course they're sexist and all that, but I think children should have what they really want, if it isn't something dangerous. I still think my mother was imposing *her* values on me, and that wasn't fair.

We learn what we care about.

And so we are already raising issues: How do parents make value choices? What risks do they take? Some other students are eager to launch into a discussion of Barbie dolls. I think about it and make an arbitrary decision: This sharing will generate lots of discussion, but we can't have it all right now. You may ask questions but not give opinions, today. Keep a list, though, to go in your folder: What issues raised today do you want to have a discussion on later? Which passions of other people inspire *your* passions?

This is the beginning of the emergent curriculum process. Within my broad definition of the boundaries of child development, I want content to reflect students' own interests, what they care passionately about. If I believe this to be an important developmental principle—we learn what we care about—then I not only have to talk about it, the class has to be an example of it.

And so if I ask people to list things they want to talk about, then it's important that I follow up and make sure that happens. That's how trust is built.

We go on around the circle. What do children care passionately about? An amazing variety: dill pickles, a tiger kitten, a grandmother, a lavender blanket, puddles after a rain. One student cared passionately at age 2 that she did *not* want her baby brother, and she made several attacks on him. Shock on the part of several members of the group, and another child development issue clearly raised.

Twenty people have talked. I ask them to take a break and do either of two things:

1. Write in response to what someone has said that really set you off. Just express your feelings, whatever they are, what you wanted to say but I wouldn't let you. OR

2. Go talk to someone who said something you want to react to. Tell her/him what you're feeling.

Fifteen minutes. Some animated conversations, other people writing. Some ignore both options and stretch, go to the bathroom, get coffee, pull out knitting. That's OK too. I use my own physical rhythm and my teaching experience as the basis for guessing what time structure will work for people. As teacher, my attention span is invariably longer than that of many students, who are less invested in the class than I. I have to respect their need to tune out at intervals, without assuming that everything that happens in my class is so important that they should be paying attention every minute. I could insist that they maintain the semblance of paying attention, but that's all. I'm not willing to do that; I'd rather give permission for honesty.

Back in the group. Can I risk continuing this activity through all 35 people? I think so. We've gotten going, and everyone needs a turn. General interest feels pretty high. People are saying interesting things, and they have a diverting variety of styles. If I were lecturing, I'd expect them to be able to pay attention to me, one style only, for at least an hour. We've had some variety in structure. I introduce a bit more variety by going back to the dots on the name tags, since they've had some more informal time together: Have you figured out what the dots mean?

What's purple?

That one is easy, as are dark blue and black; nearly everyone got those. The rest were harder, but we talk about them. No one exactly got the west/east side of town, but one small group came close. Some people love the challenge of games like this; others clearly didn't get into it.

Back to sharing passions. Several repeats, two passes, then a shocker:

> I cared passionately about my stepbrother. He was 10 years older—I was 11—and I wanted him to hug and kiss me. I used to sit on his lap and grab his hand, and after a while I guess he decided I meant it, because he started sneaking into my bed at night. I was pretty sure that was bad, but I liked having him play with me, even though he hurt me sometimes. Then my dad caught him and there was an awful row and my stepbrother moved out. I cried and cried.

She bursts into tears. The rest of us sit stunned. I wonder, have we established such trust, so quickly? Or does this student, whom I don't know yet, need to try to shock, to get attention? Or did it just burst out, and now she'll wish she hadn't told us and be ashamed to come back? Her neighbor puts an arm around her, and I'm grateful. I say gently, "Thank you for trusting us enough to tell us. Children's passions aren't all harmless, any more than adults' passions are. Some teachers and parents feel that strong feelings should be suppressed because they're dangerous. I don't believe they can or should be suppressed, in most instances, but I agree that whenever someone cares very much, there is risk involved. And so we need to be aware of that and help each other, and children, deal with feelings."

The student gets up and leaves the room, sobbing. There are two students who haven't talked yet; they choose to pass. And so I ask people to write: What are you feeling now? React to what anyone else has shared. What was the best thing that happened for you in today's class?

The worst? When you're through, put everything you've written in your folder, your name tag, too, and you may leave.

There are 20 minutes left in the session, but we've done enough. I had planned to ask them to list at least five group members' names, too, to let them know I'm serious about that, but it seems like too much now. Next week. A few people spend the whole 20 minutes writing.

To my relief, Berta, the student who left, comes back soon afterwards. I put my hand on her arm. "Thank you." "Was that all right, to share that with this group?" "Are you OK?" "Yes," she assures me, "I'm in therapy and I've talked about it before. I wanted to let people know that this happened to me. I can handle it. I just cry when I talk about it."

3
Covering the Content

What *is* the content of child development? I do want students to learn theory, to learn it so well that they can use it. Because I want more than rote learning, I try to include only a few concepts in any course, to give time to zero in on a concept from varied angles. Increasingly it has become clear to me that learning requires redundancy—many opportunities to take a concept and mess around with it, apply it to one's own experience, ask other people about their experiences, ask more questions, write and talk about it, assimilate it.

When I teach child development, what I'm really trying to do is to enable adults to understand what it's like to be a child. I also want them to get a handle on the idea of *development*—an orderly process of growth, marked by a series of developmental tasks to be confronted and mastered. Because these tasks have been defined in somewhat different ways by different theorists, I can choose, as a teacher, which ones to emphasize in my course. I do so on the basis of the depth of my understanding of them, as well as on my view of their importance. It's important that I teach from my own strengths; and since the potential content of child development, as of any subject, is infinite, there's no way I can cover it all, so I don't have to try. I teach from my own growing edge, taking off from my questions, knowledge, and excitement to trigger others'.

The notion of *covering*, incidentally, has nothing to do with learning. It means only that I have salved my conscience by exposing students to all those important things, through lectures or reading assignments. That's no guarantee that they have learned them. I care about what students really learn, and I have no illusion that all the students in any course will learn all the same things. Nor should they.

As David Hawkins has made clear:

> We are profoundly ignorant about the subtleties of learning but one principle ought to be asserted dogmatically: That there must be provided some continuity in the content, direction, and style of learning. Good schools begin with what children have *in fact* mastered, probe next to see what *in fact* they are learning, continue with what *in fact* sustains their involvement. (Hawkins, 1970, p. 40)

In Hawkins's words, "The variety of the learning—and of inhibition against learning—that children bring from

The notion of *covering* has nothing to do with learning.

Bob Herbert

What I'm really trying to do is to enable adults to understand what it's like to be a child.

17

N

Name-dropping is not what beginning students need to learn.

home when school begins is great ..." (p. 40). Adults, even more than children, bring a wide variety of learning experience to a class. If I agree with Hawkins, I must therefore individualize, providing choices which enable each student to experience continuity in her or his learning.

In this course I have decided to emphasize these developmental concepts (not necessarily in this order):

developmental tasks
trust, caring, and vulnerability
separation and object permanence
autonomy
classification
initiative
industry: accomplishment and failure
conservation

the context for development
motivation and learning
getting stuck
family and culture

This is my selection from Erikson, Piaget, and others. I will mention the names of these theorists, but I don't believe that name-dropping is what beginning students need to learn. Rather, I think they need to acquire a sense of the relevance of these concepts to their own lives, as people and as potential teachers.

What are all the ways people might learn about child development? How shall I get them into it? To get started, I invent activities, prepare reading lists and handouts and mini-lectures. I don't preplan week by week. The class calendar is posted, to give students as much predictability as possible, but some events may get filled in only a week in advance. My biggest challenge at the beginning of a class is to explain its structure clearly, while enabling students to get acquainted with each other so they can provide mutual support and resources. I need to get them into it and establish, from the start, a dependable feedback structure to ensure that both they and I know what's going on.

I have no course outline. Instead, for my own planning, I have a theme folder for each of the concepts listed above, full of assorted notes, activity ideas, handouts, references, and so on. I keep adding to them, and I reread them to refresh my thinking. I begin with the concepts, but I can predict that there will be some changes of emphasis along the way, as students respond to my ideas and each other's.

I don't worry about teaching facts, except incidentally. While facts can be learned through reading or being told, they won't be retained unless they're functional for the learner, answering a question the student has already asked. They are best learned through experience; so I ask students to observe children and pay attention to the assorted facts they acquire this way.

I do, on the other hand, teach skills. In this class they include (1) making increasingly detailed observations of child behavior, (2) making increasingly complex generalizations and inferences from observed behavior, and (3) becoming increasingly competent in written and oral communication. Skills are learned through practice, so I need to provide many opportunities for students to observe, listen, talk, and write.

It's session three. Where are we? We have shared passions and raised a variety of issues, many calling for follow-up. I have my list of basic concepts—in my head, so far, not given to the students—which I would like to cover. Just as in preschool, my task becomes one of taking each individual's interests and experiences seriously while giving the class a coherent focus. And so I keep trying to interweave the emergent curriculum with my definition of what child development is supposed to be about.

In my view, it's irresponsible for a teacher, even a beginning teacher, to take verbatim anyone else's definition of what child development is about, to teach the syllabus

It is irresponsible for a teacher to teach the syllabus or the textbook uncritically.

or the textbook uncritically. Teaching is a personal act. The often lamented state of contemporary education is, I believe, a testimony to the extent to which teaching at all levels has become depersonalized—rationalized, teacher-proof, constantly monitored by tests. I would much rather risk idiosyncrasy among teachers than noninvolvement in either their subject matter or their students.

In suggesting such subjective criteria for course content, I guess I am assuming that the teacher is a person of integrity and knowledge. Not, perhaps, always true. But I am a believer in self-fulfilling prophecies; teachers are more likely to be trustworthy and competent if they are trusted. In chapter 12 I talk about trusting students' potential. I think it's important to trust teachers' potential too.

I think I will risk, today, introducing a new topic from my curriculum—trust—and then relating it to the issues of passion, caring, and vulnerability. And I want to try several activities which contribute to redundancy, helping students to get a handle on this concept from several different angles. Writing, again, serves as a beginning focusing activity and a way for me to continue to get to know individuals. I write these directions on the chalkboard:

Get your folder. Read notes to you. Write in response to any of my notes, if you like. Then write:

Describe a time in your childhood when you trusted. What happened?

When you're done, put your writing in your folder.

Ten minutes. Then a question to the whole group: Is it a good thing to trust, or not? How many of you think it is? (Raise your hand.) How many think it isn't? How many didn't vote? Why not? Tell us about it.

Free associate to the word *trust.* Just call out; don't worry if you're talking at the same time. (I write all their responses on the board, a wide selection.)

Discuss: Under what conditions is trust established? Can you generalize from your experiences?

This discussion, unlike the free association, gets started slowly. This is only the third session, and I can guess that to many students this sounds like a question that may have right answers, and that I will reject some of their ideas and reinforce others. They're used to this kind of discussion in school, in which the teacher already knows the answers and is fishing for them. I'll try not to fish. It's true, I do have in my head a tentative list of conditions— stability of relationships, unconditional love, getting one's wants and needs met—but I'm open to other possibilities, and if I decide to introduce any of mine because no one else does, I'll try to introduce them as mine, not as gospel. (I once had a teacher in general psychology who gave us lists of the seven kinds of X and the five conditions for Y, all clearly arbitrary, and then tested us to see whether we had memorized them. I memorized them, but I very nearly never took another psychology course. I try not to follow her example.)

I wait. I reword the question to make it more concrete and less formidable. Which of you had experiences of trusting which worked? What made them work?

Bob ventures a story about his experience. I acknowledge and comment on it. Sally offers hers, apologetically; she's not sure it's right. That gives me a chance to explain that all experiences are right; they really happened, they're facts. We look at them to see what we can learn from them. That's how we learn about children, by observing them and our own childhood experiences. The discussion continues slowly, hesitatingly. This is a large, formidable group. I wind it up with 10 minutes' worth of mini-lecture, keeping an eye on my watch to prevent my falling into the teacher's trap of infatuation with the sound of one's own words. I talk about trust as a basic task in infancy and throughout life, and about trusting as a necessary precondition for risk-taking, and therefore for learning.

It's time to break down this big group and give everyone a chance to talk. I ask them to form groups of four. Their agenda: Go around the circle and share what you wrote, or explain why you don't want to share it. Discuss: Are you a trusting person or not? Half an hour, I guess, for this. I hope we've gotten enough connections started that they'll really want to talk. The noise level goes up immediately. I regard that as a sign of involvement in learning.

I decide not to participate in these discussions. A teacher can sometimes enrich a small-group discussion but is at least as likely to slow it down. More mature, confident students are more likely to accept a teacher as a peer. But they don't know me well enough yet, and I've already talked a lot today. I sit between a couple of small groups and eavesdrop a bit, trying to keep track of involvement level and when things start to run down. This never happens in all groups at the same time, so I decide to introduce the next activity group by group, as they seem done. It's a trust walk. Get a partner from your small group. Shut your eyes while she leads you around and out of the room, keeping you safe while providing you with a variety of sensory experiences. Then trade; you lead her. When you're through, talk about it. Did you trust her? Why or why not? I end up participating in this one myself, to make the pairs come out even. I get a different perspective on how my ideas work when I join in rather than just observe.

Turning everyone loose like this will require bringing them back together again. One or two may even go home early when they get outside. That has to be all right with me if I choose to teach in an active-learning structure. It's their choice, to come to class or not, to come late or leave early. I do my best to make the class interesting so they will want to be here. But I'm not only teaching *about* trust, I'm demonstrating it. I have to trust their own motivation to learn. Of course I risk losing some students that way. But I risk losing some students no matter how I teach. I believe trust is a better condition for learning, with students of any age, than mistrust.

As a final writing activity, I ask them to look at this issue. Write in response to two questions:

> **A** teacher can sometimes enrich a small-group discussion but is at least as likely to slow it down.

Are you a trusting person? Whom and what do you
trust or not trust?

Do you like to learn new things? Describe yourself
as a learner; give examples.

Is there any relationship, in your experience, between
your answers to these two questions?

One of the most important concepts in early childhood
education is the child as active learner. Children learn
through play—through action. Early childhood educators
knew this long before Piaget said it; we learned it by being
with children and observing what they did. It was nice, of
course, to have a research scientist verify our understanding, but we knew it first. "To understand is to invent," says
Piaget. We invented it for ourselves.

Now we teach our adult students all about Piaget. True,
they need to know his name, but it doesn't really matter
if beginning students can distinguish accommodation from
assimilation. (I have trouble with that one myself.) What
they really need to understand is the concept of active
learning; they need to know it "in their bones," which is
where they must have theory in order to be able to apply
it. That sort of understanding doesn't come from telling—
for adults any more than for children. It comes through
action, and reflection upon action. For most learners,
action needs to be something more than reading a book,
though reading may contribute to the process of reflection. How can we provide action for adult learners?

I invent activities, with the intention of turning Child
Development into a laboratory course. Some courses are
traditionally taught as laboratory. In praticum/field work/
student teaching you get to work with real children and
learn by observing and interacting with them. In early
childhood curriculum courses, especially when the focus
is on art, music, movement, or science, there are nearly
always materials available for students to mess about with,
to explore and ask questions, and to discover at first hand
what it's like to play with these things and what can be

4

$\mathbf{A}$ctive Learning

learned from them. In these courses the data are right there, and you learn by doing.

Theory courses, on the other hand, are usually taught from books. Interestingly, they are often viewed as more important and more serious than lab-type courses. That's part of the academic tradition, I guess; though no one seems to suggest that physics or anatomy labs are less respectable than lectures. But those are hard sciences; they don't have image problems in the academic community. Early childhood does, and so it often succumbs to the need to defend its academic respectability. One of the ways to be respectable is to lecture about theory.

I want students to *do* theory instead. To be a respectable teacher, in my own definition, I need to know a lot but not teach it all. Teaching it all overwhelms students and is a form of showing off. I keep reading for my own knowledge, not simply to tell students what I read. My preparation is largely indirect; if I have a lot in my head, I can pull it out whenever a question comes up, discussing ideas with students whose experiences are making them think about child development. If some of the experiences have just been shared with other members of the group, they have more immediacy and the dialogue is likely to be livelier.

One of the major concepts I'd like them to understand is *classification*—the logical ordering of one's experience. We've already played a classification game, the one with dots on name tags, although I didn't tell the students that's what it was. I might do that today, at our fourth session. So we're going to play some more classification games because games are a form of action, and thus are likely to be more memorable than words alone.

Here they come. They're no longer as silent at the beginning of class as they were the first time we met. People are glad to see each other; conversations spring up. I allow some time for them, just as I would in a class of children. I don't start exactly at the officially scheduled hour; or rather, the action starts as people arrive, but it

T o be a respectable teacher, I need to know a lot but not teach it all.

24

doesn't all emanate from me. I have chosen, as a teaching strategy, not to be in center stage all the time. I want it to be clear to students that their agendas are important too, and that a class has social functions as well as content functions. A few students resent this flexibility; they don't want to waste any time. They're usually compulsive note-takers and not interested in making friends here. I recognize their priorities but choose not to go along with

Adults as well as children do learn by playing with each other, not only from the words of a teacher-expert.

Marvin Washington

them; plenty of other classes are organized to meet their needs perfectly. This one is different. My concern is with the students who welcome a more relaxed pace, those who are rarely comfortable in more formal school. I want prospective teachers to know, in their own experience, that adults as well as children do learn by playing with each other, not only from the words of a teacher-expert. I'm modeling what I think a teacher of children, or anyone, can do and be.

Of course, once you let them talk you have to interrupt to get them to be quiet. Right. That's another useful skill for teachers. I wait for a general pause in the conversation (sometimes I can't find one) and then raise my voice. I have been known to say *Roar* and explain that I am roaring at them. Observing in elementary classrooms, I often wince at the limited vocabulary that English offers for addressing a group of learners. *Boys and girls*—now why is gender distinction relevant in this instance? *Children*—OK for the youngest, but not, I think, for fourth or fifth graders. *Class*—impersonal, implies they're all one lump. (My elementary school penmanship teacher used to call us *Little people.* We really hated that. When we got to junior high she said to us, "Little people, you are big people now.") To adults I have been known to say *Group,* or *People,* neither of which I like; *Hey,* which lacks something in politeness; *Hush,* which, idiosyncratically, I mind less. *OK.* Given the range of possibilities, I am rather fond of *Roar.* Our words do matter. If I say, "OK, let's get going," that implies that nothing important has been happening up to now. As I have already explained, I don't want to give that message. Nor will I flick the lights—memories of too many schoolrooms. I am willing to use my loud voice and repeat myself, and laugh about it.

OK. Take a piece of paper (there's scratch paper on the table if you need some) and fold it in half. Now in half again. Now in half the other way (I'm demonstrating). Now in half that way again. Now open it up and see if you have 16 sections marked by folds. Now, tear them apart along the folds. It doesn't matter if you do it neatly.

Now you have a pile of little pieces of paper. You will need those and a partner for the next step. You'll need a small work space for your papers; either turn your chairs to face each other and work on your laps, or move onto the floor.

Each of you working independently, sort your papers into three or more piles. Put the ones together that go together, however you want to define *go together.*

When both of you are done, explain to your partner how you did the sorting. What criteria did you use for each pile?

Report from your pair on one criterion you used. I'll list them on the board. Lots of possibilities!

Let's try something more complicated. Join another pair to make a group of four. You'll need a shared work space.

Each of you take five things out of your purse or pack or packet. Put them all together in the middle of your space. Invent a way of sorting them. All of you need to agree.

Now invent another way of sorting them.

Now another.

Report back to the whole group; I'll list your categories.

What kinds of decisions did you have to make?

This has been a long and complex activity, raising a variety of good questions. I suggest they take a break.

Bruce Jennings

Children are more likely to remember the connections they make for themselves than those they are simply told.

Mobility increases; people go to the snack table, go out into the hall, stretch. Many people are continuing to talk about the activity.

Time for a mini-lecture. I explain that we have been classifying. I mention Piaget. I talk about language learning, the fact that all language is a series of classifications. I ask if any have spent time with a child learning to talk, and if they can tell us how that child classified animals, or people, or foods, or other things. Several nice stories; people do pay attention to children's so-called mistakes in naming things. I ask if those who are familiar with other languages can think of anything which is distinguished in one language but not in another. Someone remembers learning in an anthropology course that Eskimo has many words for snow, and Arabic for sword. People are making connections. I comment that children are making connections all the time, and that they are more likely to remember those they make for themselves than those they are simply told.

I ask them to do a homework activity with a child. (Does anyone not have a child handy? Can anyone else volunteer one? You can work with a partner if you like. We match up a few pairs of people.) Provide a collection of miscellaneous materials and ask the child to sort them, using whatever words you think will be clear. Take notes. Write a description of what happens, including:

the items

what you said

the child's age

what the child did and said.

Bring your description, and your collection, to class next week.

There are 10 minutes left. Time for one more game. I say, Reach out with your hand and touch something blue, something on another person. [This is my own modification of "Touch Blue," from *Playfair* (Weinstein and Goodman, 1980). I invented it on the spot in a class one day, where we didn't have room to do the original version.

The authors of *Playfair* encourage you to invent your own games, and to involve members of the group in giving directions, as I did here.]

Surprise, confusion, laughter. They do. I do too. Some find they have to move; that's fine.

Keep touching your something blue, while you reach out with your other hand and touch an ear that isn't yours, on a different person.

Crazy. Lots of awkward positions, but more expressions of pleasure than pain. Let go of your something blue, hang onto the ear, and with your other hand touch a toe on someone different.

I give another direction or two, then say, "Someone else give a direction." No one does. "You're all stuck in this position until someone else gives a direction." "Touch something long." A few more. "Let go!"

I ask, "What have we been doing?" (A right-answer question. Usually I avoid those, but this one seems easy enough to risk. It is. "Classification.")

Right. We played another classification game 2 weeks ago, remember? They do; the dots.

When I was in sixth grade my teacher taught us the difference between Doric, Ionic, and Corinthian columns (we were studying Greece), and for weeks I went around classifying columns on buildings. I still do. Think of something you're going to look for on the way home: triangles, or birds, or white-wall tires, or Volkswagens, or whatever you can get into. See what effect it has on your awareness of your environment.

And all semester, whenever you see a child, try another classification task: guess how old she or he is. Pay attention to what cues you use. Confirm your guesses whenever you can.

When they arrive the next week there's a sign on the board: Find a partner (someone who wasn't your partner last week). Find a work space. Get out your collection of things and give your partner the same instructions you

5

Space and Time

gave the child you worked with. See what happens. When you're both through, write about it in the same way you wrote about the child. Put both observations in your folder.

(If you forgot to bring your collection of things, find a pair of people to observe. Write your observations.)

This will take awhile; I have some time to observe and to think. As I watch them spreading out their miscellany, I am reminded that active learning demands *room*, in both spatial and temporal terms. If I'm going to tell you about my childhood and hear about yours, we need to be able to move our chairs so we can see and hear each other comfortably. If we're going to play games that involve movement, we need a space that is more than wall-to-wall desks. If I give people a series of complicated directions like those with which I began today, I can only guess how long they'll take to complete the task, and I know for certain that some will take longer than others. I have to think about orchestrating all this and perhaps providing some alternatives for those who finish early. Again, that's more like teaching children than giving the conventional college lecture, in which everyone is doing the same thing at the same time.

I am moderately satisfied with the room in which this class meets. It's carpeted and the chairs are movable. Considerable effort over time by me and other like-minded faculty has gotten couches and cushions, as well as hard chairs, into our classroom space. People have choices of where to sit, and we can move the furniture depending on what we want to do. In this large class there are not enough straight chairs to go around, which is fine with me; that makes it clear that varied seating choices are appropriate. I sit on the floor myself if I'm not speaking to the whole group. I want people, adults as well as children, to experience *mobility* (Jones, 1973) in a learning environment, not just to assume that learning is a sedentary, silent activity. I don't want prospective teachers to assume that they have to learn how to make children be quiet in order to teach them. For myself, I rarely stop

Active learn-
ing demands
room.

I don't want prospective teachers to assume they have to learn how to make children be quiet in order to teach them.

side conversations if they occur during a large-group discussion; they don't bother me, and they often represent active involvement in a related issue. Respect for the group means remembering to whisper; it doesn't demand constant attention (often faked attention) to a single agenda.

I want my classroom to contain elements of *softness*, of sensory responsiveness, which enriches experience and relieves tension. The typical college classroom is hard: hard floor, hard desks, bare windows. Students are expected to sit upright and remain physically separate from each other. Here we have some soft seating and we encourage relaxed postures; we bring food and drink to share, and people may touch each other.

If I want the social structure of a class to function effectively, I have to take spatial organization seriously. I did this at our first meeting, when I told the members of one small group that their circle wasn't round. I learned to be authoritative about details like this by observing a sixth-grade teacher who had 35 children in her class and a firm commitment to group problem solving. It's hard to make a circle of that many people with no one in a second row; and, in fact, in her classroom the circle had to be a square or it wouldn't fit in the space. She patiently insisted that the children learn to come together in that square, teaching them north, south, east, and west as guides for moving their chairs in turn. She was convinced that this organization mattered and was willing to take as much time as necessary to achieve it.

Before I met her, my own tendency had been to ask people to make a circle and let them be sloppy about it. And I have watched other teachers ask their classes to form small groups and have some students position themselves outside the circle and, invariably, outside the discussion. If it is OK with me for some students to be nonparticipants, then this kind of self-segregation is permissible. But generally it is not OK with me, so I have learned to be direct about my expectations: "That isn't a circle. You need a circle so that everyone can be part of the discussion, so people can see each other." And I'll wait until it happens, helping as necessary.

Not only spatial organization, but also *timing* becomes a major issue as soon as you start breaking a class into small groups and providing opportunities for people to do different things at the same time. I rely on experience in estimating how long an activity will take. My plans for a class session often include marginal notations indicating time spans. I nearly always make changes in midstream, typically eliminating something I planned to do because something else is taking longer than I expected.

Having posted a calendar in order to make things predictable for students, I have some obligation to stick to the schedule; but I also have an obligation not to extend things beyond their usefulness and, conversely, not to cut things off when they're going especially well. I have to be willing to *let go* of some of my good ideas without making a fuss. As a listener, I am invariably annoyed when speakers keep explaining that they have to rush because they're running out of time, or that they are leaving out some things they had planned to say. They may well have to leave out some things, but they don't have to keep telling me how much I'm missing; that doesn't contribute to my learning, it's just an ego trip for them. When I omit, I try to keep my mouth shut about it. That 's *my* decision, not something to be laid on the students in order to impress them with how much I've planned.

> **W**hen I omit, I try to keep my mouth shut about it.

It's a matter of taking responsibility. Because I believe that learners learn best when they make choices, I try to provide many choices. How a group is structured and timed, however, is its leader's responsibility. I ask for frequent feedback from students, but I make the structural decisions for the group. Somebody has to, and I trust my judgment in this instance more than I trust a majority vote. I observe carefully. And I might ask, trying to decide whether it's time to move on from small-group discussions, "How much more time does your group need?" But since each group is likely to be different, the decision is still mine, and I have to be willing to be authoritative about it.

While I keep my mouth shut about omitting content, I do share timing issues with students. I am modeling being a teacher for them, and the question of timing is as complex in working with children as it is in working with adults. I want them to know that. I want them to see me struggling with it, to pay attention to their own feelings when interrupted, and thus to develop empathy for children who experience interruption. I want them to know that with all my years of teaching experience, I'm still learning how to

L
earners
learn best when
they make
choices.

do it. That, it seems to me, gives them a realistic picture of the profession—its joys and frustrations.

So here we are. By this time most people are writing. Patty, who has finished, comes over to ask me a question and we talk for a few minutes. I look around, decide to say "You have 5 more minutes to write." As a teacher of young children I learned to give 5-minute warnings before transitions, to indicate my respect for their involvement and to help them start to change gears. I do the same with adults.

We're back together. "Any comments?" Several people want to talk about their experiences with children and with adults.

When that seems finished, I look around the room, name a dozen people, and ask them to stand together in the center of the room. What's the name of this group? I ask. It's pretty obvious when they're all together, and we've played the dot game before. "People wearing tennis shoes."

I ask them to stay there while I call more names and another group forms. What's the name of this group? "People wearing sandals." The third group, then, will be all the people wearing neither tennis shoes nor sandals; I ask them to stand together, too.

Then everyone sits down, and I draw three circles on the board, labeling each with the name of a group. It's easy as long as the groups are mutually exclusive, I explain.

Now, I need three volunteers to form new groups. You can call names or just move people. The volunteers come quickly—this might be fun—and I whisper *red* to Bob, *glasses* to Sally, *skirts* to Anne. Form your group, I tell them, but don't tell people what the rule is.

They proceed. Pretty soon there seems to be some confusion; Anne and Bob are arguing over Patty, who is wearing a red skirt. I intervene and suggest that everyone look around and name the groups. They do. Now, there seems to be a problem with Patty. What shall we do with her? She decides to stand between the two groups, since she belongs to both. A couple of other people also over-lap, including Joan, who wears glasses and a sundress and red earrings. What shall we do with her? Logically, she ends up in the middle of everything.

Again, I ask them to sit down. I write new labels in the circles on the board and then ask what to do with Patty, Joan, and friends. "Overlap the circles," suggests some-one. I do, and the result is a Venn diagram. I mention its name, in passing, and then say that when I was teaching a primary class we often played this game in morning meeting. The kids took turns calling names. But we never did more than one attribute at a time. Does anyone know why?

Kids would get mixed up, wouldn't they? someone asks. I agree. I launch into a short lecture on Piaget's concept of *conservation*, and that children's ability to classify is limited by their developing mental structures. Children who are not ready to keep two attributes in their heads at the same time are not ready to learn to read, as a rule, or to understand various math concepts. You can't hurry this process; it's based on accumulated experience.

A tangent discussion, which seems to me important, arises about early reading. Kathy's niece is 3 and can name lots of flash cards. I take advantage of the oppor-tunity to explain Piaget's distinction between social and logical learning. Kathy's niece can learn words by rote—social learning—just as young children learn to count by rote. But that's different from figuring out the logic of reading, just as a child who can count by rote may not be able to count objects accurately.

I have to interrupt this discussion; my neighbor has just arrived with her 7-year-old and her 4-year-old, at my in-vitation. Another question of timing; I had to decide whether to ask them to come this week or next. They weren't free to come till near the end of our class session, so I decided on this week. Now I'm regretting it; we haven't really talked ourselves out, and I haven't explained what I'm going to do. But often it's a good idea to do first, explain later; so I go ahead.

The boys look rather overwhelmed by all the people, but they know me well and their mom is here, so we settle down together at a low table in the middle of the room. What I do with them are conservation-of-number tasks which Piaget invented (Labinowicz, 1980). It's clear that Jason conserves and his younger brother doesn't, and I'm pleased to see that the fact that Sam watched Jason doing it doesn't seem to have any influence on his answers; he knows clearly how it looks to *him.*

It's time to go. I ask the students to pick up a handout on Piagetian concepts (from Singer, 1972) as they leave, and I suggest that if they have a child handy, they might try this for themselves. We'll talk about it next week.

6

Building Relationships

It's next week, and we talk about it. Berta simply cannot believe that Sam thought there were more checkers when they were spread out: "But it's so obvious. You didn't add any." Obvious to you, yes; you're an adult. You think logically about it. Sam still relies entirely on what he sees; if the line is longer, there must be more. He can think of only one attribute at a time. Young children think differently than they will when they are older. They aren't stupid, and they aren't wrong; they are thinking sensibly on the basis of their experience so far. That's important to remember if you're working with them. Observe, ask questions, get a sense of what this child understands and when he's ready to move to a new level of understanding. But if you try to *make* him understand, he may learn your words, but he won't *know* what they mean. Teaching requires patience.

Several students have tried the tasks with children of different ages. We talk about what they observed. I make available a handout on "The Hurried Child" (Elkind, 1982), which discusses some of the implications of pushing children to learn and do more, sooner. Some of them won't agree with Elkind, but this is a course in child development, and in my view the developmental point is clear: Development takes time, it takes place in stages, and if you try to hurry it, there are more losses than gains. As

Robert Meier

Development takes time, it takes place in stages, and if you try to hurry it, there are more losses than gains.

a teacher, I teach values as well as information.

I have another value I want to share with my students: Learning is in large part a function of relationships. This includes relationship with the subject matter: Surely all of us have had the experience of becoming excited about an otherwise unlikely topic because a teacher cared passionately about it. It also includes relationships with people. I work at building relationships with students myself; if the teacher doesn't get involved with students, why should the students get involved? Some will get involved directly with the subject matter, of course. But others, the field-sensitive (Ramirez & Castaneda, 1974), need human contact to make the bridge into thinking about the subject; they need recognition as persons, not only as learners.

I want students to develop relationships with each other for several reasons: to feel safe in the group; to find peers to argue with, play with, make friends with; and to become learning resources for each other. I've been providing a variety of activities in pairs and small groups, some of them playful, to help students get to know each other. Learning is a risky business; it involves self-exposure and the possibility of mistakes, as well as giving up what you thought you knew for something different. Yet somehow it always comes as a surprise to me when I discover, usually from their writing, how unsafe some students feel.

Amy, with a history of school success, wrote at the beginning of class (and shared with me only later in the semester):

> I was feeling real pleasure in going back to school— going back to do something that had been hard for me to stay with, something from which anxieties and feelings of inadequacy had pushed me away. And then I hit the first class and the realities were all there—a room full of people I didn't know. And right from the start I had to say things to people that would make them want to listen, things that would make them feel glad I was there, not "Oh God, I got stuck with her." I don't think well when I am scared.
>
> The whole learning process becomes one of taking risks, of extending yourself from where it is safe so that there is room enough to grow. Taking the risk of sharing even a minute portion of myself with a room full of people I don't know—these people who will become important to my world in weeks to come and yet who matter mostly to my self-assurance at the

moment. The goal is so clearly to move foreward, yet each step I take is made anxiously and then self-criticized. I am determined to learn and stunned at how painful it is.

Maslow (1962, pp. 46–47) has made clear this relationship between learning and anxiety. Spontaneous growth, he says, will occur only in an environment which minimizes anxiety and maximizes the delights of growth. I work hard to provide such an environment. Yet certainly it happens, as I come to think of it, that my need to deal with my own anxiety as teacher leads me to shut out awareness of students' anxieties. I know they do that to each other. So I try to develop a structure within which trust can be built, and I try to provide enough time for it to actually happen. Teaching adults, like teaching children, requires patience.

In any class, some students are looking for friends. Some of them would like me as a friend, and occasionally that happens. But I am not, at this stage of my life, really looking for new friends. I can be most helpful by enabling them to get acquainted with each other.

Making friends has always been a recognized and important function of residential colleges. You go to college to get an education, of course, *and* to develop social skills and make business contacts and find a spouse. But residential colleges, established to serve an elite population, are in the minority. Far more American college students commute to large public institutions, and some of them never get personally acquainted with either their teachers or their fellow students. They just come to classes and then go home, or to their jobs. For them, the lecture hall—and maybe, though not always, the library—is all there is to college. They don't expect college to be exciting, or even to be related to the rest of their lives, except in a narrow vocational sense. It's just something you have to do if you want to get ahead in the world.

The college where I teach is small, but its students are commuters, and most are enrolled part time. If they don't

> **S**pontaneous growth will occur only in an environment which minimizes anxiety and maximizes the delights of growth.

Some students know more than I do about things their peers want to learn.

make friends in classes, they have few other opportunities to do so. And many would like to, even though the majority are older than typical college age. Being 35 is no longer a guarantee of being established in one's relationships; many people are experiencing drastic life changes. A college class, for some people, is a starting-over place.

I want them to learn from each other, too, whoever they are. Some of my students know more than I do about things their peers want to learn. All students, whatever their background, know things about their own unique experiences that are worth sharing. We are studying human development, which each of them has experienced first-hand. It's my responsibility to put them in touch with each other.

Early childhood is not a field with high prestige. So it is particularly important that its practitioners become articulate about what they do and why.

> So many of them are basically inarticulate. They may be great with kids, have terrific intuitions and sensibilities about what to do and even how. But policy makers want to know why. I don't like to see people mealy mouthed, unable to explain themselves from a position of strength and knowledge. Too few good people have any say-so out in the wide world. (Nancy Jambor, personal communication)

Try to teach theory in ways which have some chance of sticking.

Students won't start being articulate about theory in their first theory class. But because I share Nancy's concern, I try to teach theory in ways which have some chance of sticking, becoming one's own active knowledge. (All early childhood professionals have taken child development, but few of them have become articulate in the process.) In a lecture class only the teacher gets to practice being articulate. I need to model thinking out loud and to describe what others have thought, but I don't need to spend students' time practicing. They do. That means they need to talk more than I do. I want intellectual behavior—active critical thinking—in my class, and not just by me.

And so students do not have the choice of just listening in my classes, even though some would feel safer if they could keep silent. Making friends in class is an option, not a requirement, but being resources for each other is not an option. Everyone is expected to talk. If some students say nothing about their experiences, other students have no opportunity to learn from them. This diminishes the richness of the class, its diversity, and its members' discovery of their diversity. I want students to learn about child development as a multicultural phenomenon, and this class is a multicultural group.

Good discussions come out of what people really know.

As I have described, I often structure discussions in small groups of two to four people, asking specific questions to draw on each person's experience. I make a point of asking questions they can respond to, questions which (1) have no right answer, (2) are clear and specific, and (3) ask the individual to describe an event or feeling she or he has experienced. Good discussions come out of what people really know, from their own experience. If students are asked to discuss what the book said, most of them will be inept. If they are asked to tell each other about their own experiences, then they are experts.

People start getting acquainted with each other this way, and some of them follow up with each other after class. But many people need more sustained contact with a few other people; this is a large class, and there's no way for all of us to become a group together, as there might be if we were a dozen or so. So I am about to ask them to form groups which will meet for several consecutive sessions to complete a task.

Making friends in class is an option, but being resources for each other is not an option.

I have assigned people to these groups, rather than relying on the chances of choosing that occur when a class is asked to divide itself into subgroups. I went over the class list, having decided that five or six was a good group size for my purposes, and formed each group on the basis of diversity—who talks a lot and who is silent, who is older and younger, male and female, Black and White, and so on, trying for a good mix in each. There are five groups of six and one of five. I've made up the list and am about to post it on the wall.

The task, I explain, is to teach something to the members of your group. You may teach anything you like: something that interests you and that you know something about, or can find out quickly. You may teach by yourself or team with one or two other members of your group. Your group will have an hour to meet together today, and 1 1/2 hours for each of the next 3 weeks. It is up to you to organize your time together, within this framework:

Today, poll your group to find out what each member might like to teach. Agree on any teamings. (Teams will need to get together outside of class.) If someone doesn't know, ask questions to help her or him think about it. Plan your time together to include (1) time for everyone's teaching, (2) time for group members to write a reaction to each session, and (3) if you like, a final wrap-up discussion at your last session together. You will need a recorder to make up your group calendar and a time-keeper to make sure you stick to your agenda.

To do a little clarifying: What comes to mind when you hear the word *teach*? Free associate and I'll write it down.

They do. I get a long list, in which a view of teachers as authorities, experts, tellers, is predominant. I decide, on the spot, to ask for another free association: to the word *learn*. A more varied list. How many of you like the idea of teaching other people in this class? I ask. A scattering of hands. Would you like it better if I reworded it and used a phrase like *help the members of your group learn something*? Some head nodding. OK; use whichever you are more comfortable with.

Do you think of me as a teacher? General agreement. Then I want to make two more lists: What things have you seen me doing in this class? And what things have you—learners—done in this class?

We make the two lists simultaneously. I encourage them to use verbs, *doing* words, when they start overgeneralizing. When they seem to be finished, I draw a line at the bottom of each list and ask if they can add teacher or learner behaviors which haven't happened in this class but which they've experienced elsewhere.

I ask them to keep these lists in mind when they think about what they might teach. Think especially about *how* you might teach—what you might do, what you might ask the members of your group to do. Can you teach without using any words, for example? Do you want your

Stephanie Feeney

I want intellectual behavior—active critical thinking—in my class, and not just by me.

43

learners to sit still or move, to listen or talk? Do you want to give information, or ask questions, or lead a discussion? Can you learn while you teach? What style of teaching might be most effective? Which style will make you feel most comfortable?

At the end of each task group session, each of you needs to put written feedback in your folder to help me keep in touch and to help you reflect on what is happening. Today's feedback needs to say (1) what you're going to teach, (2) how, (3) when, (4) alone or with whom. The recorder also needs to put your group's calendar up on the bulletin board. After today, you need to write a reaction to each session; I'll give you a form for this so you can remember the questions.

Now, for a transition activity, while we're still in the large group: Stand up. Make a circle, a tight circle. Drop hands and turn and face left. You will find a back and shoulders and neck in front of you. Massage them. (Murmurs of pleasure, relaxed expressions.) Turn around; massage the person who has just been massaging you.

I slip out of the circle and post the task group lists. These are your groups. Get together and decide where you're going to meet. We will not come together as a class again today, but you do need to put your feedback in your folders. I'll be circulating. If you have questions I'm available.

Curiosity (which group am I in?) and confusion. Questions. I hand out reaction forms. They look like this:

Date: Who taught?

Topic:

What did she or he do? Be specific (about actions, not content):

What did you do? Be specific:

What did you enjoy most?

What bored, confused, or frustrated you?

Did you learn anything? If so, what? How do you know?

One group comes to me to explain that they want to go out for coffee together but then what should they do about their feedback? I'm delighted. I ask if any of them will be on campus later today, or tomorrow. They check; yes, Joan will. Fine. Joan, you collect everyone's papers and your group's calendar, and leave them in my mailbox. Off they go, happily. Three groups settle down in different corners of the room. Another goes out to sit on the steps. I've lost track of the other group, but they can come look for me if they need me.

It is useful, I have learned, to ask clearly focused questions when I want to help students focus their thinking around a particular topic. In this instance I want them to provide feedback to each "teacher" and to me about how the process is working. I want them to think about teaching and learning in terms of specific behaviors rather than vague generalities, thus all my word listing today, and this follow-up. Especially, I want to communicate the fact that teachers and learners behave in many different ways. I have been trying to model this idea in class; I want them to know that that's what I'm doing, and to think about it in other settings.

Thus the homework I'm about to give them: Within the next 3 weeks, observe two different classes of children, in a school or preschool. List the things you see the teacher doing. List the things you see individual children doing. Comment: Is the teacher teaching? How do you know? Are the children learning? How do you know? Your lists should be objective: What is actually happening? Your comments will be subjective: What do you *think* is happening for the children?

Again I'm trying for redundancy: Observe me in this class, observe each other in your task groups, observe children and teachers in schools. How do teachers and learners behave? What inferences can you make from their behavior?

I want them to wrestle with the questions: What is learning? How do you know when it's happening? Which have

45

major implications for the planning and evaluation of learning settings for children and adults? This whole issue is one I've thought a lot about, and I have clear ideas of where I'd like to go with it, so I'm asking clearly focused questions. (Sometimes, in my teaching, I introduce a topic that I'm just beginning to explore. In that case, I ask more general questions, to give us all a chance to formulate the possibilities.)

No matter what or how you teach, learners will respond in diverse ways.

If they choose, I will give the task group teachers the opportunity to add one or more questions to their form— things they particularly want feedback on. And I will copy all the responses to each of the teachers and put them in their folders. (Students are free to look in each other's folders, and I could suggest they do that instead, but this gives them more assured feedback.) And because I want to communicate another important principle—that no matter what or how you teach, learners will respond in diverse ways—I plan to chart on a large sheet of paper, from week to week, the main points from everyone's feedback (anonymously).

Complicated, but worth the effort, I think.

A last question: Is teaching/learning an appropriate part of the content of Child Development? Does it belong in another course? I choose to think not. If we don't learn, we don't develop. Piaget's developmental theory is used by various educators as the rationale for their curricula. Engelmann (in Green, Ford, & Flamer, 1971) has commented that Piaget's is not an educational theory at all; it doesn't tell us what or how to teach. But I believe that the nature of teaching and learning is a developmental as well as an ideological issue (Katz, 1975), and many of my students want to be teachers. They will be putting into practice whatever they learn about child development. This is another opportunity for me to teach my values, those which are rooted in my understanding of child development. That's what I'm doing here.

In the second session of this class, we each described a childhood passion. And I asked people to write in their folders: What issues raised today do you want to discuss? This, and their writing on the first day (Write one question you'd like to discuss in class), was the beginning of the emergent curriculum process, which builds on students' own interests in order to engage their passions, their motivation to learn.

7

Emergent Curriculum

If I ask people to list things they want to talk about, I have to follow up. What happened to all that? Haven't I just been ignoring it and teaching *my* stuff all these weeks?

In fact, emergent curriculum has several sources. Learners' interests. The teacher's own interests—passions, values, active concerns. The unexpected things that happen when this group of people gets together. Events in the physical and social environment outside the classroom. And the expectations of the community—the college, the profession—for a class called Child Development.

In planning this class, I began primarily with my own interests and with the topic Child Development. As soon as the group met, I started asking its members about their interests. And I have been following these up on an individual basis. I write every week in students' folders in response to everything they write; this is one of my important teaching behaviors. With some students, I get an active dialogue going; we are thinking together about topics of their choosing.

Last week, when I asked everyone to teach something, I referred again to the second session. Teach from your passions, I advised, from something you know and care a lot about, or something you want to know more about and would like a chance to bring up. What you care about now may or may not relate directly to the things you cared about as a child, and that's interesting to think about: In what ways do people stay the same? In what ways do they change?

(In forming the groups, I was able in several instances to build on people's stated interest in someone else's passion. Kathy, for example, had written at length about her reaction to Berta's sharing at the second session. I put them in the same task group. That's no guarantee that the topic will come up again. But it might, and Kathy will get a chance to know Berta better.)

Today, task groups are scheduled for the second half of our time together. I'm going to begin with another topic of my own: autonomy. This, like other topics I have introduced, invariably is responsive to some students' stated interests, and I make a point of those connections as I go along. If the subject matter, child development, is of interest to the students, and if its content is logically related to their experiences, then it is inevitable that much of the content will be covered simply in response to their questions. However, it won't necessarily be covered in the order chosen by a textbook author. That's one reason I don't use a textbook. Textbooks are logically organized, by someone's standards; individual learning is personally organized, as each *aha* generates the next question.

Individual learning is personally organized.

For this reason, I feel free to skip around in the sequence of topics discussed in class. When I made my original list of concepts to be examined, I put them in chronological order, because that's an easy way to think about child development: it starts with a baby, see, and the baby gets bigger . . . . But it doesn't have to be taught that way, especially if I'm presenting not a tidy framework for students to memorize but a series of experiences which I hope will hook into their own. And I want each experience to have a certain independence; this week isn't meaningless if you happened to miss last week. They are tied together, but not in a linear sequence. When learning about child development, one can as easily begin with a 10-year-old and work backwards, as with the embryo. Particularly if one is the parent or teacher of a 10-year-old and that's where one's questions are coming from.

As you may have noticed, in this class we began with trust and promptly skipped to classification. Why? My reasons were organizational, rather than developmental: classification was a topic I wanted to spend a lot of time on, so I scheduled it before I introduced the task groups, which are time-consuming. I put first those topics which I knew best and had many activities for, things I didn't want to have to let go. The further we get into the semester, the more I find I must let go as the emergent curriculum starts to take over.

I'm not brave enough, or experienced enough in teaching Child Development, to allow as much of its curriculum to emerge as I do in classes in Planning Environments, say, or Administration. But I am unwilling to get trapped by pressure to cover the curriculum. As another college teacher has put it,

> Teachers who try to teach too much end up with students who learn very little. And to decide what to teach must be a marriage between what you feel is important and what the student wants to know. (Barbara McDonnell, personal communication)

I begin, as any teacher must, with what I know best. And then I provide a structure in which things will move out from me, thus the task groups, each of which will have different content. That's OK. Even if I were to lecture systematically to the whole group every week, there is no way that anyone would *learn* everything I *taught.* Different students would find different content and ideas memorable, those things which connect for them and, for those who care about me, the things which they sense I particularly care about.

I don't lecture much because I believe that active learning is more effective. It's important that things *happen* in a class: interactions and doings as well as *aha's* about ideas. Memory of a concrete event often triggers memory of a more abstract idea. "I hated that trust walk," one student wrote. I think she's likely to remember, and even reflect upon, *trust.* Is trust important? Why did being dependent on someone I didn't know make me feel so awful?

Here we go with today's class and my beginning words to them: Childhood passions can serve as a lead-in to the subject of autonomy—the exercise of the will to get what one wants. This surfaces as an issue when children are 1- and 2-years-old, I explain; they are learning to use words, and one of the important words is "Mine!"

Good research begins with someone's passionate interest in something.

I describe a study done by one of my graduate students, Eileen Nelson (Pacific Oaks master's project, in process). Working with 2-year-olds in group child care, she became fascinated by the issue of "Mine!" So she observed 2-year-olds and interviewed their teachers in a dozen child care centers to see how children and adults were handling this issue. Good research, I mention, begins with someone's passionate interest in something. Eileen *wanted* to do this study. It was hard work, sometimes frustrating and sometimes even boring, as is true of learning to do any-

50

thing well; but she persisted because she cared. Children do that, too. So can college students and teachers.

I don't want to tell them what Eileen found out. I want to see if we can generate the options for ourselves, through role playing, because I think that will be more memorable than just taking notes on what someone else said (even though the someone else is my friend, and I can talk about her as a real person). I have provided a supply of attractive playthings that might inspire someone to assert, "Mine!" They include my daughter's elegant stuffed lion, a marble rollway (blocks with tunnels, enabling a rollway to be constructed and marbles sent through), a doll which wets and a bottle of water, a collection of plastic wild animals—things like that. I'm going to try the role playing in front of the whole group—risky, in a group this large, but I want to lead the discussion which follows each episode, and I can't do that if we break into smaller groups. I'm hoping that some people are feeling comfortable enough by now not to be intimidated by the group's size, and that there are some people who simply enjoy having an audience.

I explain that we are going to do some role playing of "Mine!" behavior and that I need three volunteers, two children and a teacher. Cheers; Bob and Patty and Ellen are willing. Ellen wants to be the teacher. I explain to the others, and to the group, that this is a child care center, that Bob and Patty are not yet 3 years old, and that they are, therefore, learning about autonomy.

I take Bob and Patty aside, one at a time, to explain their roles to them privately. I ask Patty to choose one of the playthings, the one she likes best, for her very own. She pounces on the lion (I do admire her taste!) and hugs it tightly. This is your new lion, I explain, and you have brought it from home to the child care center today, and you don't want anyone else to touch it. Then I explain to Bob that he can begin by playing happily with any of the other toys, but then Patty is going to walk in with the toy she has brought from home, and he is going to want it very much.

To the teacher I explain, in front of the group, that it is up to her to watch or intervene, whichever she thinks she should do, in Bob and Patty's play. There are, of course, other children in your group, but just for now you don't have to worry about them. Bob is already here and he is playing. Patty will arrive soon.

Bob settles down with the marble roll, trying to construct a rollway. The teacher, watching, sits near him. Patty enters with a flourish, hugging her lion ostentatiously. "Oh Patty, what a nice lion," says the teacher. "Is it new?"

"Mine," says Patty happily, showing it to the teacher. Bob stops playing and watches for a moment. Then he reaches out and grabs the lion's tail.

"No!" says Patty. "My wion!" Bob pulls harder. Patty hits him.

The teacher intervenes: "It isn't nice to hit. Bob likes your lion. Could you let him hold it?"

"No!" says Patty, hitting Bob again. (He winces; these role plays get realistic sometimes.)

"You need to use your words," says the teacher. Several class members chuckle; Patty *is* using her words, she's just backing them up with her fist. Bob won't let go of the tail. Patty screams. The teacher, looking increasingly anxious, pries Bob's fingers away from the tail and, fending him off with one arm, suggests hopefully to Patty that perhaps Lion can take a nap in her cubby. "No!" says Patty. "*My* wion!"

I interrupt, calling the end of the act. I ask each player in turn, "How do you feel?"

"Mine!" says Patty, stubbornly.

"You really got into that," I comment. "Do you really want that lion?"

"Yes, I love it," explains the grownup Patty. "And it's my new lion and he can damn well keep his hands off it!" The class laughs appreciatively. They aren't all lion fans, but nearly all can identify with the intensity of Patty's wanting. (I wonder privately if I'm going to be able to get it away from her to take home.)

"Bob, how about you?" He's just been role playing, nothing personal. He moves easily back into his adult self. "I don't think it's a good idea to pry a child loose from a toy," he says. "The teacher needed to use *her* words, to explain to me that it was Patty's lion."

"Ellen, how are you feeling?"

"Frustrated!" she wails. "I didn't know *what* to do. I think I'm going to make a rule that kids can't bring toys to school!" (Laughter from the group.) "I think children need to learn to share, but how can I teach sharing when it's Patty's new toy, her very own?"

The issues are certainly getting raised in a hurry. I have to decide whether to go into a discussion of them now, or wait. I decide, not too certainly, to wait. I ask the members of the group to make note of the questions they want to raise about what has just happened; we're going to do two more role plays, and then we'll discuss them all.

I ask for, and get, three more volunteers, and again explain the children's roles to them privately. This time the toy in question is something belonging to the center; Kathy is playing with it and Berta wants it. Kathy chooses the marble rollway, which Bob has left on the floor. Berta watches her for awhile, then asks politely if she can play too. (She sounds more like a 5- than a 2-year-old; I wonder if anyone will pick up on that.)

"Go way," says Kathy, firmly two. Berta watches some more.

"Kathy, Berta would like to play with you," says the teacher.

"No," says Kathy. Berta moves a little closer, encouraged by the teacher's support. "No!" says Kathy. Berta retreats.

"When you're through, it will be Berta's turn," says the teacher, hopefully.

"No!" says Kathy. Berta cries; the teacher pats her. I call time.

"How do you feel?" I ask Kathy.

"I felt fine until she cried. Then I started to worry that the teacher would make me let her play. I didn't want to play with her. I would have let her have those dumb marbles if the teacher made me; I didn't really want them anyway." (Sudden spurt of note taking from the listeners.)

"Berta?"

"I don't see why she wouldn't let me play. I was real nice. The teacher hugged me, but she didn't really help. I never get to do anything."

Amy, the teacher, breaks in. "I really wanted to help, but Kathy was being so negative, I didn't know what to do. I guess I just gave up on her and tried to make Berta feel better."

"OK, make note of your questions," I say, "and let's try one more. Who wants a turn?" This time it's Eduardo, Sarah, and Joanne; Sarah says she'll be teacher. I give Eduardo a fuzzy blue baby blanket and tell him it's his blanky, from home. I tell Joanne she wants it.

Eduardo sits on the floor, his blanket over his shoulder, twisting his hair with his other hand—a perfect picture. When Joanne attacks, Sarah is clear and firm: "Eduardo is sad, and he needs his blanky. Let's see what we can find for you."

After a little more interaction, I interrupt, thanking the players. I ask for comments and questions from the group. There are many; these scenes touched people's own experiences, both as children and as adults working with children. We talk about the pros and cons of sharing, the different ways an adult might intervene, and the different messages given to children. I ask if they think any of the children were learning not to care too much, learning that there's no point to passionate wanting because you won't get it anyway. Active discussion of Kathy and Berta. Is that something children need to learn? The group splits, between those who are sure it's never too soon to learn to share, and those who think that caring comes first and sharing later.

I tell them that Eileen found a similar split among the
child care centers she visited. Most permit children to
bring security objects, like blankets, but some, like Ellen,
have a rule against toys from home, and they require that
the center's toys be shared. In contrast, there are centers
which permit toys from home and don't insist on sharing
anything, even the center's toys, in the belief that for young
children the experience of possession helps build a clear
sense of self. Predictably, in these centers teachers spend
a lot of time in conflict resolution, interpreting children's
feelings to each other and helping them learn strategies
for getting what they want. This is an area in which different adults have different values; you get to sort out your
own.

"Question," someone asks. "Is that marble rollway a
suitable toy for 2-year-olds? Isn't it too hard for them?" I
agree; I'm glad she noticed. On the other hand, no one
comments on Berta's advanced language, and I decide
to let it pass. There is so much to be learned from an
activity like this; we can't do it all.

It's time for task groups. If we had more time, I would
have asked if anyone would like to try another scene with
a volunteer director as well as players. I am finding that
I would like to spend a lot of time on the autonomy issue,
more than I had predicted in my original planning. Having
structured the task-group time, I'm now committed to it.
But not having announced each week's topic, I'm free to
keep playing with that. I can spend more time on autonomy if it's exciting students' interest and mine, and let
one or more other possibilities go.

Given the opportunity, people are likely to share with
each other not only intellectual ideas, but also personal
anxieties and dilemmas and feelings of all sorts. Classrooms are simpler, tidier places without these things,
whether the students are 2 or 32. It can be argued that
learning about ideas happens most efficiently in settings
where feelings are arbitrarily screened out and students
learn to concentrate on their work for this span of time,

regardless of what else may be happening in their lives. I could even support that point of view, I think, but what I have been learning in my own teaching has to do with the importance of paying attention to feelings, even in classrooms. I believe that passions are basic curriculum for 2-year-olds. I believe they're basic to Child Development, too.

If students' feelings come to class, so do the teacher's. I teach from my own interests, I have my ups and downs, I respond more warmly to some students than to others. I try to balance that, to be responsible, to find a relationship base with each member of the group. But I don't have to be perfect; we are human beings together, doing the best we can. If a student expresses feelings I'm not prepared to deal with, I can say so. I'm not a therapist; perhaps you need to find someone to really explore that issue with. But I find that the writing process effectively deals with most strong emotions in this setting. Thus when Berta left the room crying, my response was to say to everyone: Write. How are you feeling right now? Personal writing has a therapeutic quality of its own, and it also enables me to follow up with individuals who want to talk privately. Unless I were able to use writing in this way, I think I'd keep feelings firmly out of the classroom—they are too scary.

8

Keeping Track of Individuals

Two of my colleagues, Liz Prescott and Bunny Rabiroff, once wrote a paper (in Jones, 1978) on the *invisible child*—the child who gets lost in a group of children, whose presence everyone tends to forget. They describe such a child as *stuck in autonomy.*

> The child who is successfully achieving autonomy repeatedly says, by his actions and words, "This is me. I'm going to do this. I'm not going to do this. . . ."
>
> The child who gets stuck in this stage experiences insufficient success in asserting himself. When the question of who's going to make the

choices arises, adult standards become so dominant that the child never really experiences a sense of power. The willful behavior by which he is trying to establish himself as an autonomous person is met by shaming, instead of encouragement. . . .

A child stuck in autonomy needs to be put in the position of having genuine choices. (pp. 127–128)

As I am teaching this class, I am becoming more and more aware of my own underlying theme for looking at child development: the process of becoming a person, of developing a sense of one's self in the world, of learning to meet one's own needs in the context of others' needs. Autonomy is a crucial stage in this process. I'm going to be redundant about it, emphasizing it for several weeks and from several different angles. It's a piece of theory I want students to gain a real understanding of, one which has major implications for their interactions with children and the decisions they must make as they teach or parent.

I am choosing to emphasize this concept partly because of my own values and partly because I have direct access to some original research on it: a basis for storytelling with the class. Whenever possible, I teach theory from data—stories about my own or someone else's firsthand experience. I could try telling Erik Erikson's stories, or Robert Coles', but I don't know Erik or Bob personally. I can tell my own stories, and I do, all the time; but on this topic they're unsystematic. On the other hand, Eileen is my friend, and so are Bunny and Liz, and they have done systematic studies in this area and talked about them with me. Furthermore, Bunny and Liz have a videotape which they will let me borrow, in which the Robert described in their article can be seen being invisible. A picture may be worth many words, and here is one that directly illustrates the words I have asked students to read. (I handed out copies of the article last week and asked that they be read for today.)

Now we watch the videotape. As usual, I have trouble with the machinery (one reason I'm often reluctant to utilize such materials). As usual, someone in the class figures it out. Then we talk about Robert at length. I helped write the article, by interviewing Bunny, so I can talk about it out of my own experience (and make it clear to students that real people write books, not just faceless authorities). We argue about the teacher's interaction with Robert and about the desirability or undesirability of encouraging the willfulness of children.

I talk a bit about the concept of getting stuck. Erikson has defined each of his stages to include this possibility; thus an infant who fails to establish trust gets stuck in mistrust, and a child who fails to develop autonomy gets stuck in shame and doubt. Healthy development is a spontaneous process; it can be counted on to keep going on its own momentum. But some children get stuck, somewhere along the way, and then planned intervention, like that Bunny has described, becomes important.

Some children, like Robert, get stuck through anxiety generated in interpersonal relationships. For them it's not safe to act autonomously; it's safer to remain incompetent. Later, some children fail in school tasks for the same reason. Other children may have physical disabilities which get in their way. Selma Fraiberg (1975) has described the development of blind babies, most of whose parents need help in learning how to respond to them in growth-promoting ways. Typically, parents of sighted children respond spontaneously to their behavior, but blind babies are an unknown quantity to most parents and they don't know what to do. They can be taught. Growth is self-motivated in the presence of appropriate stimulation.

Growth is self-motivated in the presence of appropriate stimulation.

It's important to get a sense of the normal range of development in order to be able to identify stuckness. A child who hasn't walked yet at 15 months is within the normal range; a nonwalker at 2 years is developmentally delayed. One of my own children didn't talk till he was 3, but I knew him well enough to know he wasn't stuck, just

Subjects & Predicates

We need to learn to value each child as we discover, and contribute to, her or his imperfections.

resisting. (At 23 he talks just fine.) Another child this age might have had reasons for his speech delay which suggested intervention. There seem to be critical stages at which tasks are best learned; pushing to learn them earlier has little effect, and too-long delay can make them harder to master.

Lots of questions. Parents' desire for the perfect child is mentioned. I pontificate a bit: We need to learn to value each child as we discover, and contribute to, her or his imperfections. The human condition is not to be perfect, and to come to terms with our pain.

We are not done when we hit the time scheduled for task groups. We stop anyway; that's a commitment. I ask students, for next week's discussion, to observe a child standing her or his ground. We talk a bit about what that means—another way of describing autonomy. Remember Patty and Kathy in the role play? Were they standing their ground?

They go to meet in their task groups. I settle down, within eavesdropping distance of one group, to read their folders. Sometimes I circulate from one group to the next trying to be an unobtrusive observer. At other times, like today, I catch up on another teaching task and leave them to themselves, trusting the peer process. Reading folders in a class this big takes a lot of catching up. But I've had enough experience teaching with folders that I can't imagine giving them up; they're how I individualize my teaching, keeping track of each person in the group.

There are invisible students in nearly every college class. Within the limits of my energy, I'm no longer willing to have any in mine. In a class of 35, even in a class of 15, I can't possibly keep track of everyone through conversation and group discussion. So writing becomes mutually functional, a means of one-to-one dialogue. In some of my classes I also provide opportunities for peer dialogue in writing. In this class I'm concentrating on teacher-learner dialogue.

And it *is* dialogue. My students are my peers, in an important sense. They have valid experiences which I, they, and others can learn from. I share mine and insist that they share theirs. I respond to everything they write with ideas of my own. Sometimes their words don't trigger very much in me, and all I can manage, in the margins, is a *yes*, a happy face, an *I agree*. Sometimes I have questions about what they've said, so I write them down. (Some students answer them, others don't.) And sometimes, the best times, I am moved to write at some length about my own experiences, my ideas; to think out loud in their margins, sharing with an individual student a unique piece of me. Of course, some students are more able than others to elicit this depth of response in me; so they're the ones who get my best as a teacher in this mode—writing. With a few, the correspondence thus begun continues for years afterwards; we have discovered that we like thinking together.

Not all students are comfortable writers, therefore I don't invest all my teaching energy in writing. I structure my classes so that I am providing for learning in a variety of modes. Students have opportunities to listen to short lectures, read, role play, watch a film, and engage in small- and large-group discussions. Some of them will learn the

> **I** respond to everything they write with ideas of my own.

most from me, from my words, written or spoken, or from their observations of who I am. Some will learn the most from the author of a book they choose to read; some, from another member of the group, perhaps through the formation of a lasting friendship, or perhaps only through the impact of a story told by the other. Some may benefit most from experiencing the process as a whole, and themselves as active learners, or from having the responsibility of providing a learning experience for a small group of peers.

In contrast, to design a course so that all students are exposed to a single set of stimuli, in my opinion, seems as arrogant as to design an evaluation procedure which ranks all students along a single continuum. The teacher who behaves this way says, in effect: I know what all of you must learn, I know how to teach it to all of you, and I can find out whether you have learned it. Or perhaps she or he is merely saying: I don't care about teaching all of you, only those who learn the same way I do. This class is for sorting students, not for teaching them all.

What do students write? I've been asking students to write every week, mostly during class time. Students wrote feedback at the first two sessions, and they are doing so weekly in their task groups. I have asked them to comment on others' shared passions, to write about their experiences with trust, to make notes on adults' and children's reactions to classification tasks. Some of them are also writing about their reading; others haven't gotten around to it yet.

Because I have a good idea of what some people are doing and thinking (those who talk or write a lot) but am uncertain about those who make themselves less visible, I'm about to ask for another, more systematic piece of writing: a mid-semester self-evaluation, in which I ask students to list the reading they have done and plan to do, reflect on their small-group teaching experience, assess what has and hasn't been useful for them in class so far, and comment on what hasn't happened yet that they want to have happen. I want to know how it's working for them, not for *them* as a group, but for each individual. And I want their input in planning the rest of our time together.

9

Observing and Reading

"Did you see any children standing their ground?"

Yes, they did, and it's storytelling time. Assorted examples of the "Mine!" variety—they really do know what autonomy looks like—and also, to my delight, some more complex examples which lead us beyond autonomy to the next concept I have in mind.

Joanne describes, in lively detail, a scene in a sandbox. A 4 1/2-year-old named Maria was in effective charge of the action. She was making sand cakes for a party, molding damp sand in a shallow cup, and turning it carefully onto a plank table, then decorating each cake with leaves, twigs, and a sprinkling of dry sand. She dealt skillfully with a series of potential interruptions: a boy who wanted to eat a cake ("No, the party hasn't started yet, but I'll save that one for you."), another girl who wanted to make a

I can't imagine teaching child development and not asking students to spend some time observing children to get first-hand data related to the ideas we talk about.

Subjects & Predicates

bigger cake with a pie pan ("We need them all the same size at this party. Use this cup."), and an accident with a passing truck that demolished part of a cake ("That one wasn't very good anyway. Here, put the rest of it in your truck and I'll make a new one."). At last the party really took place, with several satisfied celebrants.

"*Is* that standing ground?" asks Joanne. "It's much more complicated than all those children saying 'No!' but Maria was certainly getting what she wanted."

"Yes, I think so. It's a fine example of what Erikson calls the stage of *initiative*, in which a child learns to make complex choices and carry them through. Maria is exceptionally competent. She's altogether different from Robert (in the videotape, remember?), who was also 4 but who hadn't ever learned to act on 'This is what I want to do and this is how I'm going to do it.' This is high quality play, with a great deal of physical and cognitive and social learning going on. Maria has learned to set herself a task, to deal successfully with frustrations along the way without getting sidetracked, and to achieve satisfying closure for others as well as for herself. That's a lot to learn in 4 years."

I expect students to have active-learning experiences in class, to reflect on their past experiences, and to keep getting new input outside of class sessions through reading and observing. I can't imagine teaching child development and not asking students to spend some time observing children to get first-hand data related to the ideas we talk about in class. Observing, in my view, is the first and most continuous thing a teacher needs to do; teaching begins with children, not curriculum. Again, a bias I freely share with my students.

Similarly, I want them to read. Books are high among my passions; I would like students to become excited by them, too. For this reason, and others, I don't use textbooks. Looking back over my own years of schooling, the only textbook of which I can remember either title or content is Katherine Read's *The Nursery School*. It is significant, I think, that it is the shortest textbook I was ever assigned. And it's full of concrete examples, and when I read it I was having my first experience in a nursery school and I needed to know exactly the things it talked about.

I remember many other books I read, not textbooks, though I can't usually remember for what class or on whose recommendation I happened to read them. When and why did I first read Erikson's *Childhood and Society*, or Lois Murphy's *The Widening World of Childhood*, or Frances Hawkins's *The Logic of Action*? Was I a graduate student, or a working teacher? No matter, I've been thinking with them ever since. And so in my classes I can hope that each student might discover at least one personally memorable book, and the joy of reading, if not previously discovered. Nobody reads textbooks after they leave school, though they may use them as references occasionally. I'm interested in establishing reading as a continuing, self-initiated behavior, not just something you do because your teacher makes you.

A textbook gets in the way.

In some classes I have tried assigning books, or having groups of students agree to read a selected book, and scheduling book discussions. That seems to work well for many of my colleagues; it works for me only sometimes. If I want all of us to have a common piece of writing to discuss, I find it more productive to provide a short handout. I've done that several times in this class. "The Invisible Child," which provoked the most thoughtful discussion, was supplemented by a videotape by the same authors.

At the beginning of this class I provided a reading list. It should have been annotated, that sparks students' interest better, but I didn't have time this semester. The directions which went with it were:

Browse through this list. See if there's anything on it that you've been wanting to read, or a title that intrigues you.

64

Copies of some of these are in the book box and may be checked out in class. All of them are in the library and some are in the bookstore.

Choose one and begin. Don't keep reading a book if you find you can't get into it. Return it and try again. These are all books I have found meaningful, but you're not me. The book has to speak to *you.*

Read at least two books during the semester. Write comments, brief or longer, on your reading. What ideas do you agree with? Disagree with?

Have you had any similar experiences? Put your comments in your folder for response. You don't have to have finished a book to start writing about it.

I've read all the books on this list, so don't summarize the content of a book unless you're doing so for yourself to keep. However, you are not limited to the books on this list. If you read one that isn't on the list, tell me something about the content and about your personal reactions to it.

In fact, I want students to read more than two books; and it has been my experience that most will, once they get interested. If I *require* more than two, a few will start looking for the shortest. I've tried to put together an interesting list: some case studies, some fiction, some theory. Accounts by teachers, therapists, parents, novelists. Several storybooks for school-age children, good reading for adults as well.

Some students are frustrated: What *should* I read? I don't know what they should read. I can make friendly recommendations, and I suggest they talk to their friends. For a student who really wants a survey of the field, like Bob, who is a graduate student with teaching experience, I will recommend a textbook. He wanted to check out the gaps in his knowledge; he isn't a beginner in the field, needing to be turned on by it. Texts are for review and reference, not for turning on.

I bring my own books to class and let students borrow them. I lose a few, but not many. That helps some people get started. Certainly I believe students need to learn to use libraries, but I care most about getting books into their hands, by whatever means. I mention books I've liked to the group and to individuals.

My other main reason for not using a textbook is that it gets in the way. If I require a textbook, students have a right to expect that we will use it in class, discuss the questions at the end of the chapter, or follow the sequence, or have exams on it, or something. I want to invent my own questions and feel free to play with the sequence. And I don't give exams.

10

How Do You Know If They're Learning?

Since last week I've read their self-evaluations and the notes from each task group. I also went back to the lists they made at the beginning of class, when I asked them what issues they wanted addressed in this class. It's been a lot of work; I didn't get much else done in my life this week. I ended up making notes on a separate page for each individual:

What interests has she or he expressed?
What have the two of us done about them?
   written dialogue
   class discussion
   reading
   teaching in task group
Here are a few examples.

Marilyn didn't list any issues. An older student returning to school, she has clear ideas of what college is supposed to be like, and this class doesn't fit them. She's the one who hated the trust walk, and she balked at choosing her own readings: "I want an overview of child development. I don't just want to bounce around." I asked if she'd prefer to read a basic textbook, and she thought she would, so I suggested she check the library and bookstore. She found one and has been reading it systematically, making conscientious notes on things she wants to remember. I also suggested she tackle Erikson's *Childhood and Society*, as an important book in the field, and observe her own children to see if his chapter on "Toys and Reasons" would increase her understanding of their play. She has done both, writing detailed observations and relating them to Erikson. In her task group she gave an illustrated lecture on physical development in childhood, taken from her textbook; she was fascinated by the changes in body proportion that occur as a child grows. Other members of her group, on their reaction forms, agreed that she talked and presented attractive charts, while they listened and asked questions. They enjoyed her enthusiasm, admired her preparation and her clarity of presentation; one said he already knew the material, but it was a helpful review.

Kathy, who wrote at length in response to Berta's sharing at the second session, has continued to write a great deal about her feelings and her own childhood experiences. She has read *Dibs* and *One Little Boy* and several stories about children written for children: *Harriet the Spy* and *Bridge to Terabithia* among them. She has been an active discussion participant. When she talked about her niece's early reading, I gave her an article on "The Hurried Child": she read it promptly and went off in search of the book. In her task group she chose to lead a discussion: "What did your parents tell you about sex, and when?" Group members found her a good discussion facilitator and a sensitive listener, and most felt they had learned about the diversity of children's experiences by listening to each other.

Eduardo's strong interest has been in the development of the bilingual child. I suggested that he read Rodriguez's *Hunger of Memory* (1982) (not on the class list but part of my own recent reading; I'll add it to next semester's list), Ramirez and Castaneda (1974) on bicognitive development, and Coles's volume on *Eskimos, Chicanos, Indians* (1977). He hasn't written very much, but he waits to talk with me after class. He participated in a role play, and he taught his task group nursery rhymes in Spanish. They enjoyed his sense of humor and appreciated his patience.

How can I rank these three students, and all the rest, in terms of the quality of their work? I don't try to. My interest is in initiative, intrinsic motivation, individual differences; if these students become teachers I want them to take these things seriously in children. So each of them needs to experience being taken seriously by me, their teacher. Whereas some of them have had many experiences of being acknowledged and valued by other people, others haven't; and most haven't had much such experience in school. When they in their turn become teachers, they're likely to revert back to all their accumulated

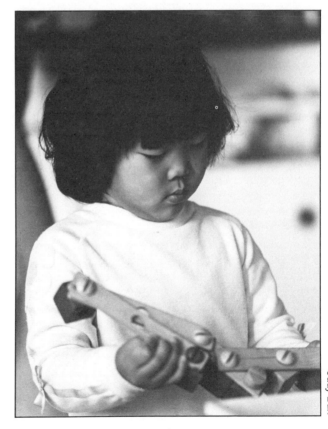

My interest is in initiative, intrinsic motivation, individual differences; if these students become teachers I want them to take these things seriously in children.

Judy Burr

pictures of *teachers* and how they behave—unless I'm able to make this other model real for them, something they have appreciated and would like to provide for other learners.

That won't happen for everyone. Probably not for Marilyn, though I have made a point of acknowledging and meeting her needs. She enjoyed being an A student in a traditional system; she resents the fact that the rules of the game are different here. I, on the other hand, experience this as the best of all possible worlds because I don't have to grade students. [After years of complaining about the necessity of giving grades, Pacific Oaks faculty one day—nearly 10 years ago—decided not to. We write narrative evaluations for each student, a process to which the student may contribute. (For a brief discussion of grading, see Chapter 18.)] So I don't have to compare them in any way, and that frees me to value each as an individual, without the constraints that grades would provide for either them or me.

Probably not for one or two others, either—Alice, maybe. She doesn't say a word in class and she turned in a very sketchy self-evaluation. She read a picture book to her task group, without comment; they weren't sure what she was trying to teach them. My written questions to her have gone unanswered; I'll have to ask her to come talk to me. I haven't been doing a good enough job of keeping track of her; inevitably, that happens with someone.

Thinking about the class as a whole, how do I know if it's working? I use three criteria:

1. *Energy*

How much energy is being generated in the group? I look for percentage of people talking, evidence of active listening, noise level, facial expressions, body postures, interrupting (as positive evidence of excited thinking), how long an activity goes on, how hard it is to get it to stop (Do people object to being interrupted by me?). I see high energy as evidence of high morale and active learning.

High energy is evidence of high morale and active learning.

2. *Direct feedback*

I ask for feedback from every individual, nearly always in writing. Oral feedback offers less privacy and so it yields less variety of response. I ask specifically, What's working for you? and What isn't? I make it clear that I assume not everything is working, in order to give students permission to express the negative. That's riskier than saying nice things.

3. *Individual involvement*

Involvement is reflected in the quantity and quality of work done, in terms of communication, skill learning, and abstract thinking. In traditional classes specific products are required: Students are tested on their understanding of reading and lecture material, and/or they must write papers on assigned topics. In this more open structure there is more room for choice, and for goofing off.

To earn credit, students must: (1) Communicate effectively about what they are doing and how they perceive the class. (2) Engage in practice of the skills most critical to the content of the class, in this class, observing and communicating. (3) Show at least minimal competence and growth, as appropriate, in these skills. And I expect students to be able to make increasingly complex generalizations and inferences from their observations of child behavior. This process implies some application of theory in making inferences, and some awareness of the whole range of possible explanations for behavior. It builds on observation skills and uses skills in written and oral communication.

Required production sometimes interferes with the thinking process.

Some students produce far more than they would if faced with a set of detailed requirements; others produce less. But the chances are that they *think* more; required production sometimes interferes with the thinking process, because it forces it into a limited time frame which may not match its rhythm. Assignments and deadlines are often useful for getting things done, and I wouldn't want a world in which there weren't any. But I think a balance is necessary, and I'm willing to provide the other side of it.

Because I have little interest in the sort of learning that prepares people to pass a test, I don't test. I ask people to do things and to write and talk about them, and I judge the quality of their learning by the energy with which they communicate about it. Quality is different for different students. In this class, Joanne does high quality thinking which I respect as a peer; I learn from her insights. Kimiko isn't my peer in this arena but she's right in there thinking, relating the new ideas in this class to her wealth of practical experience as a child care director. Unlike privileged, bright young Joanne, Kimiko isn't used to being a critical thinker, but she's eager to learn. I would hate to grade the two of them. Kimiko has accomplished far more in her life; she knows how to *do*. Joanne is a skillful player of the school game, an abstract thinker; she doesn't have much real-world experience. How can I value one of them more than the other?

Coming into the room today, students encounter these written instructions posted near a couple of boxes of small blocks of varied colors and shapes, my collection of pattern blocks and Cuisenaire rods:

Find a partner.

With your partner, select a dozen blocks for each of you. You should each have an *identical set.*

Sit down on the floor, back-to-back. (You can lean on each other if you're friendly.)

The partner taking the first turn begins to build a structure with her or his blocks, giving the partner verbal instructions so she or he can try to build an identical structure at the same time. Don't peek.

When you're both done, you can peek. What happened?

Now it's the other partner's turn to give instructions.

Soon the room is full of back-to-back pairs. I wasn't needed as a partner today, so I circulate to see how it's going. As the quicker pairs finish, I suggest they find another pair to observe: Do they do it differently than you did?

Back in the large circle, I ask:

How many of you did it perfectly?

How many didn't do it perfectly but thought you did a good job?

How many think this is something you're not very good at?

Those of you who think you're good at it, how did you get to be good at things like this?

Some discussion follows, with people giving both general and specific explanations. Then I ask the rest: How could you get better at it? "Practice." Why would you want to? "Well, if you were going to grade us on it," says Gordon. I store that one away to bring up again a bit later and ask them all to get out a piece of paper and make a list, just for themselves, of "10 things you do very well. Or just well, if you run out of verys. After you finish your list, write for each item: How did you learn to do it?"

Then I put two headings on the board, *what* and *how*, and explain: "We're going around the circle. When it's your turn, tell us one thing you know how to do well, and how you learned it. I'll make a list." They do, and I do. The *whats* include cook, teach, whistle, play the cello, crochet, garden, read, make friends, make love; the *hows* include read cookbook, observed good teachers, practiced, asked questions, wanted to, fell in love. As we get toward the end several people pass; all theirs have been listed already. At the end I ask, "Did any of you have any *hows* that aren't on the list?" A few; I add them.

"Now, if you look at the list of *hows*, how could you classify them? What are the main ways people learn to do things?" We mess around with that a bit. One, we agree, is from teachers, both people and books. The people may tell us or show us. Another is through practice, doing it over and over again. We have trouble classifying *wanted to* and *fell in love*; finally I suggest that they have to do with motivation, and that competence in some things is not so much a matter of information or skill practice, it's spontaneous involvement. Ellen comments that most learning happens through a combination of all these things, and I agree.

Another question: "Did anyone list walk, or talk, or eat with a fork, or tie your shoes?" No one did. "Did anyone list *anything* you learned before you want to school?" Yes, Joanne learned to read before she went to school, but not well, she decides. "Why not? Aren't those things important? You do them very well, don't you?" "So well that we take them for granted," Sarah volunteers. Those are things we do all the time; we don't *think* about doing them.

Time for a mini-lecture. We're talking about learning, I explain, and the ability to keep on learning is probably the most important human characteristic. Many animals don't learn much; they just do what they're genetically programmed to do. But young mammals, especially the human kind, don't survive unless they are both fed and taught by adult members of the species. There is no humanness in isolation; we are social creatures, and we continue to need each other and to learn from each other all our lives.

What are the conditions for effective learning? We have discussed two of them, which Erikson identified as the tasks of the first two developmental stages. Babies must learn to **trust**, to rely on other people. Toddlers practice **autonomy**, learning to rely on themselves as independent beings with strong wishes and desires: "Me do it." "No!" "My wion!" (A nod to Patty.) If they are thwarted too often, they experience self-doubt and may become invisible children, unable to move on to the next stage: *initiative*.

We haven't talked so much about initiative. But do you remember the story Joanne told last week, about 4-year-old Maria in the sandbox? I said then that that was a fine example of initiative: choosing a task, competently dealing with frustrations along the way without getting side-

Initiative is the developmental task of the pre-school years.

tracked, achieving satisfying closure. I *want* to, I *may*, and I *can*. Maria has learned in that setting that she *may* and she *can*. She has discovered that she is somebody, and she knows who, so now she's free to concentrate on a task.

Initiative is the developmental task of the preschool years, and the activities children engage in to develop initiative are generally self-chosen—initiated and defined by the child. We describe them as learning through *play*. In the next stage, which Erikson calls **industry** and which tends to coincide with going to school, tasks are often set by adults for the child. Children are seen as old enough to be responsible, to do things right. And so they face a new challenge: Can I learn to do this well, to meet someone else's standards? The process is generally seen as *work*, rather than play, and the possible outcomes are accomplishment or failure.

It looks to me as if most of the *whats* on your lists fall into this category. They're things you learned to do well by others' standards as well as your own, things you learned to do by working rather than playing. Do you see any exceptions? Yes, making love is certainly learned through play. "And I really learned to cook that way," Bob says. "I was living alone and no one else judged what I cooked; I just kept messing around to see what I liked, and when it was too awful I chucked it and went to McDonald's."

So there are definite exceptions, and I think they usually have to do with pleasing yourself (though making love is a mutual process). Probably it's useful here to make the distinction between intrinsic and extrinsic motivation. Are those words familiar? (Several heads shake: No.) Do you remember a little earlier when I asked why you might want to get better at the back-to-back building, and Gordon said he would if he were going to be graded on it? What kind of motivation is that? Does a grade come from inside you or outside you? (A right-answer question, which I usually avoid, but an easy one.) Outside you. OK; *in*trinsic motivation comes from *in*side you. *Ex*trinsic motivation comes from outside you; it's like *exit*, where you go out. If I grade you in order to motivate you, it's because I'm not sure the task itself will motivate you. (I'm assuming, of course, that grades will; and that's not always true.)

Now, probably some of the things you do well are things you learned because you were intrinsically motivated and others because you were extrinsically motivated: to please someone else, to get a grade, to avoid ridicule or punishment. How many of you think most of your motivation was intrinsic? Extrinsic? Let's have some examples to get this clear.

In your task groups, the task was teaching each other something. Did any of you learn anything from anyone else? (Most hands go up.) Was there any extrinsic motivation for you to learn in that situation? (No one can think of any, except that this is a college class and you're supposed to learn in it.) Is there extrinsic motivation for you to learn in this class? (Some confusion. I explain that extrinsic motivation usually takes the form of rewards and punishments. "I could flunk, I guess," says someone. "Is it possible to flunk here?" We toss that one around.) Do you learn better when you have grades and exams? I ask. (Mixed response: "I work harder." "I don't, I just try to get by." "How do you know if you're learning?" "That's what tests are for, to tell you." "But I always forget that stuff in a week.")

It goes on until I get nervous (*Is this child development? What is the relationship between one's adult experiences and one's understanding of children and their learning?*) and pull it back to childhood with one more question: The things you're good at are mostly things you learned after you were 5 or 6. Does that mean nothing important is learned before that time? Let's brainstorm (I erase the board). The question is: What do children learn between birth and age 5?

Following the rules for brainstorming, I write down everything they say, including *cry, walk, go to the toilet, eat, talk, say please, stay out of the street, ride a trike,* and lots more. I ask those who want to argue to wait until we have the whole list. I add one of my own, *walk on uneven ground,* since I have vivid memories of taking my assorted-age kids hiking up a creek and of me behind, dragging the 2-year-old who kept stumbling over the rocks, while the competent 4-year-old leaped on ahead. That stimulates a few more complicated ones. When it's done, we're open to argument. "Babies don't learn to cry; that's inherent." "So is eating." "Well, sucking is, and I guess chewing is, but using a spoon is learned." We keep sorting out.

Then the next question: What do children *do* to learn these things? This is another list of *hows;* this time try to make it all verbs, behaviors, as we did when we were discussing teaching and learning before the task groups started. What does a child learning to walk *do?* From Marilyn, who has a 1-year-old: "She pulls herself up, and she falls down, and she pulls herself up, and she lets go, and she falls down, and she pulls herself up, and she lets go and she doesn't fall down, and then I give her my finger to hold and she takes a step, and she falls down ... and one day she takes a step all by herself, and that's the beginning." And how do you know she's learned to walk? How does she know? "Because she walks!"

Is child development a body of knowledge or a set of skills?

What does an adult learning child development do? Is there any parallel with the child learning to walk? How do you know if you've learned it?

We've been sitting in the big group for too long; I see one near-sleeper and several wigglers. Stand up, I say abruptly. Touch the ceiling (how close can you come?). Touch your toes (or your knees, if your toes are too far away). In that position, turn around twice in place. Stand up, with your arms outstretched (carefully)—are you touching anyone? If you are, take hands. If you aren't, move to where you can. Holding hands, walk across the room. Turn back-to-back and rub that person's back with your back. Turn face-to-face, and say something friendly. Move to the nearest chair (don't sit down!). Holding on to it, stand on one foot. With the foot that is in the air, touch someone else, gently. Take that person's hand and follow me. Grab other hands as they wave by.

I move in a large circle around the room, followed by a long tail of people. I make my circle smaller and smaller until we're a snail, all tightly coiled around each other in the middle of the room. I stop and don't say anything. Silence and closeness. Then someone laughs, and several more get the giggles, and I suggest it's time for a break. Take 10 minutes to make your body comfortable, I advise, and to start thinking about the questions I just asked. Either write about them, or talk about them with someone else.

There's too much content in this session, I realize, and I've probably talked too much. My mini-lecture seems to have become maxi. I've introduced concepts of initiative and industry, play and work, intrinsic and extrinsic motivation—too much to remember. So I'll need, as usual, to provide redundancy. I have a handout for them on learning through play and work, a paper I wrote to try to sort these ideas out for myself and later incorporated into a book (Jones, 1973). And I'm sending them out to observe again, preschool children engaged in sustained, involved social or dramatic play—examples of initiative. I ask them to observe a child involved in a self-chosen task and describe: What is she or he doing? (objective) What are her or his goals? (inference). I want them to look for *quality* in play and to think about what they mean by that. I'll also make sure that all these concepts come up again during our next few class sessions.

They've been reflecting during the break, I hope, and so have I. I bring the group back together. (It would be better to provide variety in structure at this point, to break into small groups for discussion, but I find I want to keep my finger in this pie, to have the final word, if you will. That's OK if I don't do it too often.) I repeat the three questions I asked just before the break. I make it clear that I'm after another list of behaviors: Learning child development, what do you *do*? Observe, read, talk, think, listen, play, work. . . . Is there any parallel with the child learning to walk?

Disagreement on this one. Anne argues convincingly that they're different sorts of things, that walking is something you practice until you've mastered it, and then you just *do* it. "But you keep elaborating on it," says Marilyn. "You learn to walk up and down stairs and on uneven ground (a grin at me), and you learn to run." "Yes, but it's still clear what you're doing and when you've learned to do it," Anne objects. "It won't ever be clear when I've learned to child develop." Laughter. "Is child development a body of knowledge or a set of skills?" I ask. "Can competence in child development be described as behaviors, as verbs?" That's tricky. It generates more disagreement, which continues until it's time to go.

11

Empowering Learners

The longer I teach, the more I come to define human relations in terms of *power*. My son in college takes issue with this concept; he says it's mechanistic, machines have power, people don't, and we shouldn't use mechanistic metaphors to try to understand organic processes. He may be right, and we both enjoy the argument. But I go on using it because it's a stronger word than influence, or control, and I appreciate the power (!) of strong words in helping myself and others understand what really goes on in relationships between individuals and groups.

Eve Trook, a college teacher who was once my graduate student, has helped push me toward this understanding. I'm a slow learner, and it has taken me a dozen years to get around to trying some of her ideas with my students. But last year I did. And I found her role play so effective in bringing up most of the crucial issues in the exercise of power between adults and children that I'm going to try it again in this class.

She defines the uses of power in ways that have proved memorable for my students:

Power exercised ON a child means that the child has no real choice, i.e., the child is *oppressed.*

Power exercised FOR a child means that the child is provided experiences that contribute to the development of self-esteem and confidence that lead to power for the child, i.e., the child is *facilitated.*

Power exercised WITH a child means that teacher and child are equals learning together, and the child acquires new power, i.e., the child and teacher are *liberated.*

The critical difference between FOR and WITH is teacher control. Power used FOR the child means the teacher is intentionally guiding, structuring, or supporting toward a goal. Power WITH the child means both teacher and child share a sense of wonder and are creating together. (Trook in Jones, 1983)

Strong words. Eve uses them deliberately, as I have come to do. She believes adults need to become aware of the ways in which they interact with children, so they can make conscious choices of what they do. I agree. And so we'll try the role play. I'm using role playing in this class more than I have in my teaching before; I've always been a bit scared of it. But I'm getting braver, having taken the risk and had some successful experiences. We all grow that way, a little at a time.

This role play, rather like the last one we did, begins with teacher and child, one child this time, and play materials, and instructions to the child to help guide her or his response to the materials ("interested in materials," "interested in socio-dramatic play," "interested in language," "interested in sensorimotor experience," "interested in social interaction with teacher," "not interested"). There are also three judges, official observers who will be asked to describe the interaction in terms of the three power categories. Everyone has received a handout, abridged from Eve's article, describing these [see Appendix]. Sally volunteers to be the child, but it's harder to get a teacher; being "judged" sounds formidable. Finally Gordon agrees to try.

Gordon chooses a card—"Legos," gets the Legos from the shelf and puts them on the floor. Sally chooses her card—"interested in social interaction with teacher," and shows it to everyone but Gordon. Then she settles down on the floor with him. He asks if she'd like to play with the Legos—"See, they're red, and white, and you can build with them. What would you like to build?"

Sally ignores his words and looks at him provocatively, fingering her hair. "Did you know I got a haircut?"

Gordon: "Did you? That's nice."

Sally: "Yes. Do you like it? I went with my mommy."

Gordon: "Yes, it looks very nice. Now, what would you like to build? See, you put them together like this . . . ."

Sally: "Do you like my green ribbon? My mommy put a green ribbon in my hair because I got a haircut. Did you know I got a haircut?"

Gordon: "Yes, you just told me. I like your ribbon. Did you know you can build a house with these Legos? What does your house look like? Does it have windows?"

Sally: "My baby sister's hair is real short. It isn't pretty like mine. She's just a baby."

Gordon: "Yes, babies don't have as much hair as big girls do. But her hair will grow. Does your baby have a bed? Could you make a baby bed with the Legos?"

The interaction continues in this vein until time (3 minutes) is called by the judges. It's the chief judge's task to ask first Sally, then the other judges, whether power was used on, with, or for her. Sally is clear: "The teacher really wasn't interested in my haircut, though he pretended he was. He was only interested in those Legos. I didn't want to play with them; I wanted him to pay attention to me. I guess that's power ON." The judges agree.

Gordon explains. "She really wanted to talk about her haircut, and I did respond to that. But I kept trying to find

a way to get her interested in the lesson. I was supposed
to be teaching her about Legos."

"How did you know that?" someone asks.

"I drew a card, and it said *Legos*," Gordon explains.
"So that's what I was supposed to teach, and I was trying
to be a conscientious teacher. Was I doing it wrong? She
was a nice little girl; I would have enjoyed just talking to
her. But I was the teacher."

That, I explain, is the dilemma teachers face all the
time. There is a *curriculum*, usually described in much
more complex detail than the simple word *Legos*, and
the teacher is supposed to teach it. If the child isn't interested, a power struggle ensues. Who won this power
struggle, do you think?

General agreement: "Sally." Anne demurs: "But she
didn't win it very well. She refused to play with the Legos,
but she didn't really get the teacher involved in what interested her. It was sort of a standoff; nobody won."

Why, I ask, was it important that the curriculum be
Legos rather than haircuts?

The discussion which follows raises important issues:
adult authority, child autonomy, sequential curriculum,
and the possible outcomes of power struggles: Who wins?
I mention Eve's point that power is not finite: It isn't necessary that one person get it and the other person lose
it. In some situations new power is created for both par-
ticipants, out of their mutually satisfying interaction.

What did the child learn? I ask. Did she exert initiative?
Would you call this quality play? We talk about these
questions and then go on to two more role plays.

In the second, Carol as child draws the card, "interested
in materials." The materials turn out to be miniature people and furniture, and the teacher, Anne, puts them on
the floor without saying anything. Carol promptly begins
arranging rooms and putting the people in them, talking
to them. Anne just watches until Carol asks her where
the daddy is. Anne looks at each figure. "Is this the daddy?"
"No," says Carol, "that's the grandpa. He came to visit.

A child using
initiative is em-
powered.

Jerry Bushey

Thrivers are children who generally get a lot of positive teacher attention, because they help teachers feel successful.

Where's the daddy?" Anne: "Maybe he went on a trip and will be home tonight. Do you think he'll be in time for dinner?" "Yes, and we're going to have turkey. Here, you take mommy and cook it . . . ."

"What kind of power was this?" the chief judge asks Carol.

"She was nice; she played with me. She wasn't laying any power on me." "Power WITH?" asks the judge. "Yes," says Carol. Another judge has a question: "Did you feel she was intruding on your play by adding her own ideas?"

Carol hesitates for only a moment. "No, I asked her a question. And she had a good idea; I liked it. If I hadn't liked it I wouldn't have invited her to play."

The third role play involves Ellen as a child who is "not interested." She just sits, playing with a button on her sweater. LaVerne asks her gentle questions: "Did you see these new markers?" Ellen shakes her head. "What color do you like best? Shall I draw you a picture?" No response. "If you don't want to talk to me, can you point to the color you like best?" Ellen: "I don't like any of them." "I guess you don't want to play right now. I'll just sit and keep you company."

LaVerne is frustrated when time is called. "I didn't know what to do. She looked so unhappy. I thought I ought to try to get her involved." "How did you feel about it, Ellen?" asks the judge. Ellen is slow to say anything; she's really into "not interested." "Well, she wanted me to do something I didn't want to do," she said, "but she was nice about it, and when I wouldn't, she stayed with me, and that was OK. I didn't really want to be alone; I just didn't want to do anything."

This one proves harder to figure out; all three types of power are suggested by the judges. They decide that it isn't power ON; the child did choose not to participate, and the teacher honored that choice. And it isn't power WITH; they weren't creating anything together. That leaves power FOR, they decide a little uncertainly. The teacher was supporting the child toward a goal—involvement— even though she didn't succeed in involving her.

I ask my questions again, and we agree that the child learned that it's OK not to do what the teacher wants you to do, but that she was passive rather than exerting initiative. "Is this an invisible child?" someone wonders. We don't know without knowing more about her. If she is, then Bunny's strategy would be to exert power FOR in giving her choices, getting her involved in spite of herself.

It's easiest for teachers to experience power WITH when the child takes initiative and gets actively involved in what the teacher has provided. Carol is a thriver, in this sense; thrivers are children who generally get a lot of positive teacher attention, because they help teachers feel successful (Prescott, 1973). Ellen is a nonthriver, at least at this moment. So was Robert in the videotape. And teachers avoided Robert; he made them feel like failures. Teachers, like other people, like to feel competent.

I explain that I, like Eve, think that teachers who use power ON learners oppress them. So I try to avoid using power ON you, in this class. You can think about whether that's the way you experience it. When we're having discussions or written dialogues in which I'm learning too, I experience that as power WITH. Do you? This is something you might want to write to me about; I'd like to know about the way you perceive the use of power in this class. If it helps, try comparing it with some other class you've had. And if you don't share my bias, but feel that you learn best when teachers exert power ON you, I'd like to know that too. This is something I want to learn about.

Now, we're going to break into small groups to share your observations of children's play. I think there is a direct relationship between the concept of power and the concept of initiative. A child using initiative is empowered; she's doing competently what she wants to do. She's playing, and she's probably learning through play.

Make groups of four. Go around the circle, sharing the observations you made during the week. Ask each other these questions for each observation:

Was this quality play?

What were the children learning? How?

Was anyone exerting power toward anyone else? If so, was it ON, FOR, or WITH?

Did any adult intervene? If so, what effect did this have on the quality of the play?

I have a copy of these questions for each group, so you won't have to remember them all. Come get one. And I'm available if you have any disagreements you want arbitrated.

12

Trusting Students' Potential

As Gould documents devastatingly in *Mismeasure of Man* (1981), the whole thrust of intelligence testing in America, diverging from Binet's original intent of testing for remediation, has been to rank everyone on a single scale which assumes innate limits on capacity. The testing and grading process in American education, though it focuses on achievement rather than presumed innate qualities, has the same intent: to rank all students on a single scale. The content to be learned is finite; it is therefore possible to learn all of it (score: 100) or none of it (score: 0) while in the role of student. My reluctantly college-bound daughter once took an art history test on which she got an A. "That's ridiculous," she snapped. "There's so much art history I don't know at all. How can he give me an A?"

I am continually fascinated by the differences among students in their experiences, their learning styles, and their reactions to my classes. I don't think I have any business *evaluating* these differences. And yet I do it, all the time, as my egocentrism and ethnocentrism creep in. I tend to value most those students who are most like me, who use oral and written language as I do, who love to read, who share my social and political and theoretical biases. But if I act on these reactions by setting my preferences as the standard of excellence and using my position of teacher-power to decide who's a good student and who is not, then I am guilty of oppression of those students I define as nonthrivers. The role play made the process clear, as Ellen who wanted to talk about her haircut was devalued by the teacher, who had his own agenda; while Carol who wanted to do just what the teacher wanted her to do got the teacher's creative attention. In the same way Joanne, who writes detailed, thoughtful observations, and Bob, who makes particularly lucid contributions to discussions, get *my* quality attention in this class—long notes in response to their notes, conversations which I initiate because I enjoy thinking with them. Eduardo, who is less articulate in English, Marilyn, who doesn't like my teaching style, and Alice, who takes no initiative, get less than my best, no matter how I try to compensate for my gut-level reactions.

Most teachers assume that this is "the way it spozed to be," in Herndon's words (1968). I did myself, for many years; because I am the teacher, I am the standard of excellence. A professor described by one of my students was clear on this point. He began his introduction to the class with the statement that all learned knowledge is idiosyncratic but the students had better learn to pay attention to what he felt was important (Sandy Whittall, personal communication). Did he think he was being funny? I find him arrogant, if honest.

It can be argued that this is reality, that the purpose of college *is* to sort and classify people for our system as it is, and that inarticulate or unmotivated students simply won't be competent teachers and should be screened out. Adele Hanson, teaching community college students in a low-income community, and I have had an ongoing discussion of this dilemma (for her side of the story, see Hanson in Jones, 1983). I can recognize the reality of the dilemma without buying this solution in principle. My obligation, as I see it (with Shor, 1980) is not to an oppressive system but to each individual learner, whether the learner is 4 or 34. Because I enjoy the benefits of the status quo, it's difficult for me not to slip back into unconscious defense of it, blaming the victim—the student—for my own blind spots (Ryan, 1976). But I believe I am morally obligated to keep trying, to trust each learner's potential for growth and competence. I believe strongly in the power of self-fulfilling prophecies; I think students are more likely to do well if I believe they can.

People need both support and challenge to grow. In general, schools provide far more challenge than support, and the challenge is rarely tailored to the individual. I give a lot of unconditional support to help people get started, to help them recognize their own interests and competence. Much learning should be playful and exploratory,

Students are more likely to do well if I believe they can.

People need both support and challenge to grow.

and when people are in that stage of learning they don't need challenge; they need shared enthusiasm.

I do challenge students to speak up, to take a stand, to behave like critical thinkers. But I try not to confront students until I know them well enough to be pretty sure of what I'm doing, and then only if I'm willing to invest the time and energy to see them through. It's when an individual has committed herself to a serious piece of work—a product, rather than an exploratory process—that she needs serious criticism. By no means does that commitment happen for every student in my class, nor should it. I want all my students to invest energy in a class, to get hooked by it in some way, but not necessarily to give it priority in their lives.

As an example, I never correct the grammar of uncertain writers; I respond only to content. I'm a rigorous editor of master's projects, on the other hand, and of papers on which students request correction. There are standards of written English which I'm perfectly willing to uphold *when appropriate.* They do not, I believe, automatically apply to all written communication from student to teacher, and if I so apply them (as I used to, routinely), then at best I'm simply showing off, and at worst I'm intimidating uncertain writers who have something to say.

I do challenge students who I think are either deliberately or inadvertently testing limits. When there are many choices, some students may avoid choosing and wait to see what happens. The ones I start worrying about are casual in attendance, toss off brief written comments, have little to say in class. Some of them are not deliberately goofing off; this is how they have interpreted the class structure. They are right. There *is* flexibility in this class for students who are involved in it in some way. But for those who are not involved, intellectually or emotionally, then I need to make the bottom line clear. That means I have to identify it for myself. In this class I should have challenged Alice sooner than I did; she was surprised to discover that I didn't think she was doing enough.

If I were a preschool lab instructor, supervising students' work with children, I'd challenge more, because the student in that setting has responsibilities as teacher as well as learner. But not much more, not with all students. To be a learner, I think, is to have a chance to mess about, try things out, make mistakes. Practice and self-correction go a long way; my primary task is to support learning, not to correct errors. For this reason I don't give exams; and having to give grades would violate much of what I'm trying to do, because grading sets up invidious comparisons on a single standard. It is not, I think, the proper function of the teacher to screen students for future careers, but only to promote the greatest possible learning for this person at this time. (I may, as a teacher, write references for students applying for jobs. At that point I become part of the screening process.)

Like all my biases, this is one I communicate to students in a variety of ways. Today I want them to look at the diversity of their experience as members of families. They have come to know a good deal about each other as individuals; I want to keep expanding their understanding of the possible variety in human behavior, including family and childrearing.

"Am I lovable? Am I competent?" These are basic questions for children—and for all of us. Competence may be taught or practiced spontaneously. Self-esteem is based not on competence but on others' valuing of oneself. "Do I meet my family's expectations? Do they love me unconditionally or conditionally?"

As they arrive today there's a checklist to fill out, "What Is an Ideal Child?" [see Appendix], to introduce the topic of family expectations and values. When they have completed this, I say a bit about families as the setting in which children are socialized and taught who they uniquely are. Development is guided by value-laden adults, and family values are communicated not so much in words, but more often, in rituals. What did your family do together, and what does that mean to you now?

Understanding includes feeling as well as thinking. What are your feelings and memories about the rituals of your family?

Shut your eyes. Make your body as comfortable as possible. Stretch your toes, then relax them . . . rotate your head slowly until your neck is relaxed . . . then go back, in your memory, to the house in which you lived any time between the ages of 5 and 15. It's almost dinnertime and you've just come through the door. What do you smell as you walk toward the kitchen? Is it something special that your family eats? Can you smell it now? Can you taste it? Is it good?

F amily values often are communicated in rituals.

Is this meal a family celebration, or just an ordinary meal? What does your family celebrate? Who comes to your family celebrations? Do you eat together? What do you eat? What else happens? Can you remember it? See it? Hear it?

Say good bye to any visiting relatives. Do you hug them? Kiss them? Shake hands? Slap backs? Now let your memory wander to the next day, perhaps, or the next week. You and your parent are doing something together. What is it? Are you talking? Touching? Going somewhere? Working together? Is anyone else there? Is this something you often do together, or is today special?

Spend a little time together in your memory. Then, when you're ready, come back slowly to today, to this room, to your chair, and open your eyes.

This has been a slow, quiet process. Some people's eyes are still closed. Typically, guided imagery involves some people deeply and has less impact for others. Both joyful and painful memories are tapped. I wait a few minutes, than ask: Would anyone like to share what you smelled and tasted, what you did?

Slowly, people do. Poignant stories and some funny ones. We're getting in touch with a few of the things that matter to each of us. Just for fun, I ask for a quick list of everyone's memorable foods. They reflect the range of our multicultural cuisine, though hamburgers keep recurring.

Another question: I've been talking about "your family" as if everyone knows what that means. What *is* a family? I don't have an *official* definition in mind; I'm open. I don't know if we can agree on a definition, but let's try.

As a matter of fact, we don't come to agreement, but the process is interesting. I wind it up with "Who was in your family as you were growing up? Count them quickly without stopping to think about it. (Include yourself.) Now, let's see what it looks like. Did anyone have a family of two?" One person; I record that on the board. "Three?" "Four?" "Five?" "Between six and 10?" "Eleven to 15?" "Sixteen to 20?" "More than 20? How many?" The distribution of perceived-family size, recorded on the board, approximates a normal curve, with the largest number in the 6 to 10 category.

How do you define the boundaries of your family? How many of you included relatives who didn't live with you? (Most did.) Did any of you include *all* your relatives? (Only a couple did.) What determines whether a relative is a member of your family?

More discussion. Proximity of location, closeness of kinship, personal closeness, shared values all enter in. And there are some cultural definitions, too; some of the subcultures represented in the class emphasize extended family more than others do.

Take a break and write: What were your family's expectations for you? Was it clear that you were expected to be a credit to your family? If not, explain. If so, in what ways? Did you meet their expectations as a child? As a teenager? Do you now?

Fifteen minutes of writing, then into small groups to talk about what they've written. Finally, I wind up with a mini-lecture relating family expectations to the concepts of industry (Erikson) and of work and play. Different families give different messages about the values of work and play, for both children and adults. The superbaby and hurried child trends suggest a devaluing of play in childhood; childen are expected to start achieving immediately. My mother wanted me to have a playful childhood, which she had missed for herself, and I did; but both my parents modeled the work ethic, and I'm strongly caught up in it as an adult. Which do you value more, work or play? For yourself? For children?

Families and teachers may have different responsibilities in childrearing. I hand out an excerpt from Lilian Katz's article on "Mothering and Teaching: Some Significant Distinctions" (1980) and tell them good bye for today.

13

Valuing Diversity

Recently one of my students asked me, "Ideally, who would you like to teach, in order to feel you were being of maximum possible usefulness in the world?" My response was prompt, "A diverse group, in which I'm able to make them aware of each other's diversity." The question was a good, unexpected one for me, and I was both surprised and pleased by the clarity of my response.

A good mix of people has two functions: It enables peers to learn from each other, and it keeps me alert as a teacher. Diversity guarantees the constant recurrence of the unexpected. None of us can just relax and get comfortable in our sameness; we have to keep problem solving. In a diverse group I must keep learning from my students, unless I am to reject some of them out of hand. I can't just socialize them to be like me. A homogeneous group is tidier, but boring; it tends to lead to smugness on everyone's part. No one questions the teacher's assumptions, not even those who don't live up to them. They're recognized as the way things are supposed to be.

I find that having my assumptions questioned is exceedingly good for me. It shakes up my patterns of thinking and forces me to reexamine them. Increasingly I have come to believe that the *unexpected* question or comment, which is a product either of diversity or of divergent

A good mix of people enables peers to learn from each other and keeps me alert as a teacher.

thinking, has exceptional educational value. The little boy who asked why the emperor had no clothes provides a nice example. Children often do; they notice the discrepancies in our world and comment on them. We can dismiss them as just children in the effort to keep our dignity and prejudices intact, but dignity gets in the way of understanding. Working hard to maintain our image as persons worthy of respect, we lose the opportunity to see the world freshly—a view which just might expose *us* as vain and foolish, out of date, out of place, out of touch with reality. Studying child development, getting in touch with what it's like to be a child, provides us with a chance to reexamine our adult assumptions.

Dignity gets in the way of understanding.

The unexpected may take the form of the trivial, as in some of the games we play. It may be shocking, like Berta's story at our second meeting. It may be a complaint from a student: Why do I have to do that? If I don't have a good logical answer which the student agrees is logical—and often I don't—then it's time for some rethinking.

I'm usually nondefensive. I take responsibility if things aren't going well for a student, rather than laying it on the student (even if the student deserves to be blamed). While I often experience temporary hurt in the face of criticism, I don't need to express or act on it *because my real ego involvement is in the complexity of the process*, not in continuous success. Student complaints are one indicator that the learning process is working, that students are taking the process seriously and analyzing it and feeling free to be open about their feelings. And so I can respond honestly, "Is that how you're feeling? Let's try to figure this problem out."

Valuing diversity includes not having the last word. We tend to believe that the teacher should sum up whatever has been said in class, should provide closure. But that says to the students that all their contributions are only tentative, and it's up to the teacher to synthesize them into the true view. This is a real temptation, which students encourage; many of them find it reassuring to receive the word, to know that there is final truth somewhere. And teachers enjoy showing off intellectually, being admired for their charisma. (Charisma comes from the combination of competence and passion.) That inspires students, gets them started, but it doesn't sustain them in the development of their own competence and passion. *That* they need to practice for themselves.

I try to keep resisting the temptation. I may end a session with a summing-up lecture, but usually I don't. I only occasionally ask small groups to report back to the large group. Students may read books of my choice or of their own choice. And I like to provide choices during class as well, opportunities to do one thing and thus to miss something else which is happening at the same time.

We've had many small groups in this class, but until today they've all been given a common task. That uniformity undermines the goal I've just stated; I've been forgetting. Better late than never. Today begins with a choice between two panel discussions on different topics.

I've invited people to participate in the panels on the basis of things they've said in class or written about. A couple didn't want to. We've ended up with Berta, Gordon, and Joan talking about "Families That Don't Work for Kids" and Eduardo, LaVerne, and Kimiko on "Growing up Between Two Cultures." I ask each panel member to talk for 5 to 10 minutes about her or his own experience, then invite questions and sharing by others. Each panel also has a moderator, just to keep the action going.

A sign explains to the class that there will be two panels during the first hour, one meeting in our regular room and the other in the room next door. Choose the one that interests you most. If you can't choose or don't care, wait a few minutes and then join the smaller group.

They get under way. I move between the two, listening mostly, commenting occasionally. After an hour I announce break time to each group. Some people take a break; others continue to talk.

Valuing diversity includes not having the last word.

A brief lecture/discussion on culture introduces the next task. Culture is larger than family; it provides the broad context of shared beliefs and behaviors in which a child grows up. Some of the talk about roots has implied that we all need to go back to our family's ethnic traditions. But for some of us whose families are a blend of several traditions and who have not experienced discrimination based on our membership in any of them, that may not be a very meaningful task. Yet each of us has a culture, and to assume I don't is a form of arrogance: my tradition is *the* way of being human and only those other, different, quaint people have "culture." I am as embedded in my culture as a fish is in water. The fish doesn't know about nonwater unless it gets caught, and I am unlikely to recognize the distinctive elements of my culture unless I have opportunities to compare it with other cultures—other ways of being human. Living in a multicultural society and world, I must learn to make the comparison—to become aware that any culture represents only one set of many possible choices, all of them valid ways of being human.

A culture is a collection of beliefs and behaviors shared by a fairly large (or small and isolated) collection of people. Usually it has a geographic base, though there may be exceptions. In thinking about your culture, think about the largest group of people with whom you share a tradition, not a small group like your family.

How many of you can confidently name your culture and know what its beliefs and behaviors are? If you can, stand up.

About a dozen people stand. It's interesting to me that they include both people of color and some majority White Americans. A few people of color remain seated, as do many Whites. I ask those standing to identify their culture by name: Jewish, Chicano, born-again Christian, Mormon, Black American, and "just plain American" are among their responses. Then I explain that (1) those standing are to form pairs, and (2) the rest of the group are to attach themselves to a pair, creating groups of five or six. This is pretty complicated logistically; I sort them out a bit, since I want groups of comparable size.

Those of you who know what your culture is are resources for the other members of your group. The rest of you are to begin by assuming that you share a common culture. Try to make a list of its beliefs and behaviors; if you can't agree on them, that may indicate cultural differences among you. A culture, especially a complex one, is likely to include some discrepancies between beliefs and behaviors. There may be parts of your culture which you don't like, even if it *is* your culture.

You have an hour. See what happens. The small groups will report back to the large group at the end of that time; choose a person to speak for your group.

The groups move off. This task was invented by a student in one of my classes last year, when we bogged down in trying to define our cultures. I found that the process, in which I participated, contributed significantly to my own understanding; I'm passing it on to see if it will do the same for others.

By the end of the class I realize that I've included too much, again; the small group reports are rushed. Ideally this process would take longer than I scheduled for it today. I'll remember that, next time.

14

Letting Go

The only way I know to deal with being rushed—including too much material in a class—is to let some of it go. That's hard. All this stuff is important; they need to learn it in my class. How can I be accountable to the instructor of their next class, to the profession, and to the children some of them will teach, if I don't teach it all? Letting go is a recurrent life theme; Erikson talks about holding on and letting go as a dilemma faced by the young child in the stage of autonomy. How can we learn to give up some of the things we care about, in order to make room for others?

How can we learn to give up some of the things we care about in order to make room for others?

In this next-to-last session of the class, I'm about to go back to beginnings, to introduce a concept which is a developmental task of the first 2 years. Going in circles, we seem to be. But chronology isn't the only possible organizational principle for the study of child development, though it's certainly a logical one. We don't, however, always learn best the things we've been taught logically. Rather, we construct our own logical sequences, within which we find places for our experience. We tend to learn, and retain, only those things which make connections with our experience and fit into the patterns of our thinking.

Object permanence is a difficult concept for adults to understand, just as conservation is. We've moved too far beyond the child's lack of understanding; we can't identify with it any more. Of course there is the same number of objects in the row, even if they are spread out. Of course the object is still there even if it is hidden. As adults we rely on logical understanding, not just on the evidence of our senses. It's hard for us to believe that young children can't do that. In fact, it took Piaget's imaginative genius to provide a full demonstration and explanation of these differences between children's and adults' thinking.

Chronology isn't the only possible organizational principle for the study of child development.

So how to teach this concept? I could invite some babies to class, as I invited children to demonstrate their understanding, or lack of understanding, of conservation. But I've taken the easier way this time—a filmstrip, by one of my former students, which is particularly clear on the development of object permanence (Tucker, 1978).

The filmstrip comes with a discussion guide, but I choose not to use that because I want to make some other connections with students' own experience. After the film I ask for questions, and a few are raised. Then I ask if anyone has cared for a child—not your own—younger than 1-year-old recently. Several have, and I ask each: Did the baby cry when its mother left? How old was it? I start a chart on the board:

Age	Cried	Not cried
3 mo.		x

I list each baby under it. Then I raise the age limit: Younger than 2? Younger than 5? and add all the children mentioned to the chart. Then I ask, Do you see any patterns?

They don't, and neither do I. I had this good idea: I was going to use their data to show that babies younger than 3 or 4 months don't usually cry, because they don't yet have a clear idea of themselves as separate from their mothers; babies between 6 and 10 months usually cry a lot, because they know their mother is separate and they have no understanding that she'll ever come back (what's out of sight is gone); and children old enough to have achieved object permanence are less likely to cry, especially as they get older, because they understand that mother's gone but she'll come back. So much for generalizations; our chart is a hodgepodge.

I do what I generally do with adults when something I had planned doesn't work. I level with them. I explain that this is a theory which I was trying to demonstrate, somewhat crudely, with our data, but it doesn't seem to work. What explanations can they propose?

One is that the theory simply isn't a good theory; it doesn't predict things as they are. Another is that there are other variables which must be considered: the child's health, how well she or he knows the caregiver, the time of day, and so on. Another is that our sample isn't large enough for a general theory to apply; if we had 100 cases instead of 10, we might see the pattern. Good reasoning, all. I think briefly that we might try following up the other variables in these cases, decide to let it be because it feels too complicated, and instead ask another question: Is it OK for a child to cry?

Mixed reactions. We toss them around. Then, "If you look at it in terms of the power issue," I ask, "does a child who cries have more or less power than one who doesn't?"

When something doesn't work, I level with the group.

97

"More. Adults take crying seriously and put themselves out to get the child to stop."

"Less. If he used words he could communicate more effectively."

"Less. If he's crying, he'll miss out on other interesting things that are going on."

Me again: If you, the adult, were to translate the child's crying into words, what would the words be? Think just about separation crying, not crying for other reasons.

"I'm scared." "I'm mad." "I'm sad." And more.

Are those appropriate feelings to have when someone you love leaves you? Is it all right for children to express their feelings?

I go on to say that the development of object permanence is preparation for coping with a theme that recurs throughout the life cycle: attachment and loss. We learn to trust, to care, and the object of our affection goes away.

In groups of three, make a list: What are the points in the life cycle at which dealing with loss is a predictable task for most individuals? Try thinking about the losses you've experienced in your own life. Are you typical? Appoint a recorder for your group.

They disperse into their small groups. After 15 minutes, I ask the groups to stay where they are so I can call on them in turn. What's the first point your group identified? What's the approximate age at which it occurs? Then I ask the next group for their next point. Did any group have a point between these two? Following this procedure, we end up with this list on the board:

recognizing parents' leaving	8 months
choosing to leave parents for brief periods	1–2 years
going to child care*	3 months on
going to preschool*	2–3 years
birth of sibling*	1 year on
going to school	5 years

Oedipal stage: psychological loss of parent	5 years
adolescence: need to be independent	11–14 years on
leaving home	18 years
getting married*	20s on
divorce*	20s on
death of parent	40s on
death of partner*	60s on

We have starred the points which don't affect everyone. I ask: Are there losses some people experience which aren't described on this list?

death of a child, sibling, or friend

loss of health or physical capacity ("I think that one should be on the other list," someone says, and we agree.)

moving

Does predictability modify loss? Are the losses on our second list harder to deal with than those on the first (the ones that don't have stars)?

One of the parents in the class has lost a child, and she comments on the devastation of that experience. It isn't *right* to lose a child; that's not part of the pattern. It's all right to lose your 80-year-old grandmother; you'll miss her, but you've been expecting her to die.

I say that predictability is what developmental theory is all about. It doesn't give all the answers; it may not fit every child or every situation. When my children were babies I used to read the pediatrician's age-norm behavior descriptions—little handouts you got on every visit—and if they fit, I was reassured that my baby was OK. If they didn't fit, I just figured I had a unique baby. All children are unique in some things, but it can be helpful to know that behavior is age-appropriate; she isn't really getting awful, she's just turned 2. Knowledge, to some degree, empowers. People in all times and places invent explanations for what happens to them, and all explanations

Knowledge, to some degree, empowers.

have predictive power; they enable us to say, "See, I told you." In our culture we call our explanations science and pretend they're real, not invented. But scientific explanations change, just as myth and superstition do, because even in physics, and certainly in psychology, they provide only partial explanations of the way things really happen. Learn them, use them, but don't take them *too* seriously. Nothing happens *because* Piaget says it does. Piaget says it does because it happens, and he was an unusually thoughtful observer and generalizer. All of us can grow in our ability to do the same.

I want to relate the idea of attachment and loss to our discussions of culture and family. Being a marginal person, growing up between two cultures, brings heightened awareness and, almost invariably, the pain of loss. I read aloud a short excerpt from Rodriguez, *Hunger of Memory* (1982), and refer to last week's panel. And I mention the other panel, on families that don't work for kids; it may be necessary for some kids who grow up in such families to let them go, to separate in order to be a healthy adult. This is a wrenching process; often it requires therapy or some other source of support.

We're about to let go of each other, too; next week's is the last class. We'll recognize it as an ending with shared self-evaluations, a potluck meal, and a summing up: Where have we been together?

15

Where Have We Been Together?

In an emergent curriculum, I can't write a syllabus or lesson plans in advance, because I don't know at the beginning where we're going together. But I do know, at the end, where we've been. And I know that some students like to see it all down on paper, as I do. So I have written an ex post facto list of the course content containing the developmental issues we have dealt with in these 14 weeks. The list is waiting for the group as a handout, with a brief written explanation. This time I've ordered it logically and developmentally.

Child
Development
Course Content
(after the fact)

Developmental Issues	What We Did With Them	When
		(session #)
motivation:		
wanting, getting and not-getting intrinsic/extrinsic	writing, large-group sharing, lecture	2, 10
getting stuck	videotape, discussion	8
learning (and teaching)	free association, task groups, game, lecture, discussion, brainstorming, writing, self-evaluations	6, 7, 8, 9, 10, 11, 15
Erikson's stages:		
trust	free association, discussion, lecture, trust walk, writing	3, 10
autonomy	role play, discussion, video, lecture	7, 8, 9, 10
initiative	discussion, lecture	9, 10, 11
industry	lecture	10, 12
Piaget's stages:		
sensorimotor (object permanence)	filmstrip, discussion	14
preoperational (classification)	sorting objects, discussion, lecture, games, observing children and adults	4, 5, 6
concrete operational (conservation)	observing children, discussion	5, 6
work and play	lecture	10, 12
the uses of power: on, for, and with	role play, discussion	11
family and culture:		
the social context for development	value choices, discussion, guided imagery, writing, panels, lecture, checklist, small group task, story	1, 2, 12, 13, 15

Stephanie Feeney

Endings need cele-brations if members of the group have come to care about each other.

In planning this course, my underlying theme has been *being somebody in the world.* What is the process by which a child becomes a caring, competent person?

Today I have assigned everyone to four groups of eight or nine members. They have written self-evaluations, which they turned in last week. I return those today and explain that each group's members will go around the circle, sharing self-evaluations. Don't read what you've written, but talk about the ideas that have been most useful, and the one or two experiences, in class or out, that have generated the most learning. And describe your frustrations or unresolved questions. You can ask each other questions, too. Each group has a moderator/timekeeper who has been asked to try for an average of 5 minutes per person. This will take about an hour; if you have food to put in the oven, put it in now or give me instructions.

Two of the groups go overtime. The members of the others help me with food and plates. Endings need celebrations if members of the group have come to care about each other. That generally happens in a class with this much interaction. It's important to acknowledge it. Eating together is part of our celebration.

As the meal comes to a close, I explain that I like to read bedtime stories, and I'm going to read them my favorite, Kipling's *The Elephant's Child.* He was a highly motivated, autonomous, risk-taking little elephant who didn't live up to his family's expectations.

> In the high and far-off times, Best Beloved, the Elephant had no trunk . . .
> . . . And from that day to this, Best Beloved, all the elephants you will ever see, as well as those you won't, have trunks precisely like the trunk of the 'satiable Elephant's Child.

Getting a gift from the crocodile was risky. We might do some safer gift giving ourselves before we leave:

I reach down to the floor. I pick up an invisible ball, shaping it with my hands, and bounce it a few times. Then I toss it to Bob, on my left. He looks startled but he catches it. "That's for you," I explain. "You give a different gift to Patty." He thinks for a minute, then whistles in the direction of the door. Another whistle. "Come here. Here, boy." He pats an invisible animal on the head, grabs it by the collar, and pushes it toward Patty. She laughs and hugs it and gets her face licked. "My wion!" (I thought it was a *dog!*" blurts Bob.) As Patty starts her pantomime, I move quietly to three other people at approximately equal intervals around the circle, asking each of them to give a gift to the person on her left. That way we'll have four gifts going, speeding up the process.

16
Summing Up

And so the class is over.

Looking back, you'll be able to find all the gaps in this course—all the things you couldn't possibly leave out of a child development class. That's as it should be. I have already discovered some for myself, things I really must include next time. If I do, of course, I'll need to leave out some other important things. It is not OK to rush through this content, to try to cram everything in so they won't miss anything. If I do that, they'll miss a lot; real learning takes time and redundancy. Instead, I practice letting go, being a less than perfect teacher and acknowledging that fact. I am practicing attachment and loss, trust and autonomy, and empowering. And leaving room for my own growth as well as the students'.

In so doing, I am modeling the possible for those students who want to be teachers. And I am making clear both the strengths and liabilities of any program which gives learners the chance to make choices. Any choice, "I will do this," implies "I won't do that." And some of the *that's* may be the teacher's very favorites. If I can't let go of those, then I don't include them in the realm of choices; I make everybody do them. In doing that, of course, I'm taking some other risks, lack of motivation and lack of understanding among them.

For me the most comfortable compromise lies in defining what I call gross behavioral objectives (Jones, 1983). Reading, for example, is a behavior which I believe is very important, so I don't give students the choice of reading or not reading. But I don't define the behavior more precisely than that; I give them a choice of what to read. I think, of course, that every book on my list is important— they've all been important for me—but I can't expect beginning students to read them all at once. So how do I choose which ones are most important? I don't. I leave that up to them, to enable them to exercise their own judgment, to learn to read for their own pleasure and understanding. My objective includes their choosing books as well as reading them.

Similarly with writing, with observing, with engaging in class discussion. Each, I'm convinced, is an important learning behavior. So I require the behavior but leave the specific content up to the learners. They know themselves better than I know them. I respect their judgment. And I think the exercise of responsible judgment requires practice—and I want to give them some. Another behavioral objective.

Likewise, I have objectives for my own behavior. I read their writing, and I write in response. I make resources available, I talk in class (not too much), and I lead group discussions. I do a great deal of planning. I overplan; I nearly always have notes for more activities in a session than we actually do. Since I don't know in advance whether a particular discussion will go on for an hour or die in 20 minutes, I need contingency plans to feel safe, to know that we won't suddenly run out. Generally I feel most successful if I don't use all my plans; when that happens, students are taking initiative and getting involved. There is a significant difference, I find, between being irresponsible and letting go of the need to be in control. Always, to be responsible, I plan. Often, I let go of whole chunks of those plans.

I do at least as much planning after the class is under way as I do before it starts. This is somewhat of a reversal of the traditional process in which the professor writes all the lectures and prepares the exams, and then can relax between class sessions, except at grading time. I plan in advance, and then I have some relaxed time in class while students are being active; I'm not on stage all the time. But at the same time the pressure to be responsive to every student builds for me. I read and respond to their writing every week, and I need to keep track of its content in order to weave their concerns into the emergent cur-

When I don't use all my plans, students are taking initiative and getting involved.

There is a significant difference between being irresponsible and letting go of the need to be in control.

riculum. I never do this as well as I would like to; there are too many variables. In a large class some students, despite my best intentions, retreat into invisibility. The challenge is the same as that which I have faced as a teacher of young children.

In planning this class, or any class, I have found myself continually interweaving (1) pedagogical issues: What are the conditions which promote learning in a group of adults? (2) developmental issues: the content of a class in child development, and (3) teaching strategies: What shall we do together? The chapter titles in this book list the pedagogical issues I have chosen to deal with: getting started, covering the content, active learning, building relationships, keeping track of individuals—you can look at the table of contents to read them all. The developmental issues were listed first, as concepts to be taught, in chapter 3, Covering the Content; they are summarized, as we actually dealt with them, in chapter 15: This is what we have been learning about together. And I have described my teaching strategies in some detail: This is what we did and this is what happened.

I also plan the physical environment, as I do in a class of children. Student behavior is structured through the organization of things in space—play units, in a preschool (Kritchevsky & Prescott, 1969), and task instructions (oral or written), for older children and adults. Many preschools use minimal task instructions; the setting and its contents give cues for a wide range of behaviors, and a child may choose to climb, ride, paint, or dig. Within the physical boundaries most behaviors are OK. Adults intervene from time to time to set social or task boundaries. In contrast, in most college classrooms the only physical cues are: Sit down and face the front. Get note-taking materials ready on your desk. Wait for verbal instructions. A very limited range of behaviors is expected; as in *1984* (Orwell, 1981), everything not required is forbidden.

In the environment of my classes, I include:

1. Lists of resources: things to read, places to visit, people to contact.

2. Immediately accessible resources: handouts, books to borrow.

3. A structure which provides many and varied opportunities for people to get to know each other and thus become resources for each other.

4. Comfortable places to sit, in small groups as well as all together.

5. Space for active learning—movement and work with materials.

6. A calendar, to make events predictable and to provide space for people to sign up to make things happen.

7. A folder for written communications by and to each class member.

This is a story, not a model. If you try any of these ideas, they'll work differently for you. You make up your own class, for you and your students. So I haven't described everything that happened in every class. In the first place, no teacher can copy another and be effective, though all of us can certainly borrow teaching strategies and make them our own. In the second place, I'll do it differently next time; this was not an altogether successful class. I lost a few students; and some activities didn't work very well, so I'll either modify or toss them. I didn't have time to try some good ideas; I'll try them next time.

The content of this class reflects my own current interests; if I keep teaching it, it will be a different course in a few years. I find that I have to keep changing any course, partly for the students' sake and even more for my own. If I'm bored as a teacher, what does that say to my students? I find that it takes me about 3 years to get any course worked out to my satisfaction; then, having learned to do that, I need to try something new. I couldn't keep making changes, of course, if I believed there was only one way to teach child development. Developmental issues are far broader and more complex than can be dealt with in a single semester, so I choose among them. And I can make new choices at other times.

As for strategies, I try for a balance. Having thought a lot about the possibilities, I usually balance them intuitively; but from time to time I consciously analyze the balance, working from a list of possible strategies I once put together. Here's the list, and following it is a chart of the strategies I used in this class. The categories on the list and the chart don't exactly match; there are many ways of classifying teaching strategies.

Things Students Can Do During Class Time
Talk/listen
Conversation (informal)
Discussion (structured):
  in pairs
  in small groups
  in the whole class
Interview or be interviewed: ask/answer structured questions
Listen:
  to a mini-lecture (5 to 15 minutes)
  to a real lecture, by the teacher or a visiting speaker
  to student reports
  to a story, read or told
Write/read

Write:	Read:
notes on lecture	directions, posted or handouts
notes on observation	content material, in handouts or books
structured feedback	other students' writing
journal or other response	responses to one's own writing

Act/observe action
Move about within the setting:
  informal (food, conversation, using resource materials)
  structured movement or game
  structured work with materials
  structured exploration of resources in the space

Move outside the setting:	Observe in the setting:
class field trip	a class activity
structured observation	a visual presentation (e.g., film)
structured exploration or game	visiting children or animals

Suspend talking and action
Think:
  self-directed
  leader-directed (e.g., guided imagery)
Don't think: relax, meditate

Types of Activities

session	eat	lecture	game	live	media	role play	open	rounds	conversation	pairs	3 to 6	task groups	choose topic	write	imagery
		whole group →		(observe)			(discussion)			*small groups* →				*individual* →	
1	X								X	X	X			X	
2	X		X					X						X	
3	X	X					X		X_g	X				X	
4	X	X	X				X		X	X_g	X_g				
5	X	X	X	X			X		X_g					X	
6	X	X					X					X		X	
7	X	X				X	X					X		X	
8	X				X		X					X		X	
9	X						X					X		X	
10	X	X					X	X	X	X_g				X	
11	X					X	X							X	
12	X	X					X								X
13	X	X					X						X		
14	X				X		X								
15	X	X	X						X		X				

g = game

These are the things that happened during class time. In addition I asked students to make half a dozen observations and several written reports outside of class, provided handouts at some sessions and expected book reading as well—all individual learning experiences.

I try to provide a balance because different learners thrive in different structures, and because we all need variety in a 3-hour class, and during the semester. In the large group only a dozen or so students talked frequently, but at nearly every class session there was also a paired or small-group discussion, involving everyone. Asking students to write during class provided a balance between group and individual activity and insured that writing would appear regularly in their folders.

These strategies define both student behavior and my own. If I structure discussion, I can lead it, or participate in it while a student leads it, or observe it from the periphery, or do something else of my own choosing while it goes on. I may lecture, for a few minutes or more, or I may become a listener/note taker while a student reports or a visitor speaks. If students are working with materials, I may do so too; or I may choose to observe and comment. I need not be the center of student attention. Even if I have information to give, I may choose to post signs or provide handouts rather than ask everyone to listen to me. In short, I have a wide range of options for my behavior, just as students do.

Where do I get the activities I use? I invent many off the top of my head; I've invented some while writing this book. I borrow from everyone I know. I've found some books helpful; there's a source list at the end of this book. I've read all the books on the list and have used ideas from some of them.

I find I seem to have an inexhaustible fund of creative ideas once I'm engaged in the teaching process, just as I do when I'm teaching children. If I keep paying attention to the needs of learners, then I also keep playing with possible ways to teach, to introduce and illustrate ideas. It's an exciting process. I've been engaged in college teaching for nearly 30 years, and I'm more excited than ever.

17

Personal Note: A Question of Values

I have gradually come to teach the way I describe here because I'm convinced students learn more effectively, and because it's much more fun this way. This style of teaching is more work than traditional teaching, and it carries different rewards. Traditionally, the lecturer-teacher is on stage, the star of the show. Students hang on her words (and write them down); she's the source of knowledge. (When I first taught I was embarrassed when students wrote down what I said. "Don't take notes on me. I don't know what I'm saying." Later, I became more confident and enjoyed the role.) She tells them what to do, and they do it; for those who don't, she has punishments ready to hand out. It's heady, this power, and easily abused.

Why did I change my style? It's a question of values. One of the most effective motivators for change is recognition of a discrepancy between one's behavior and one's values. That's what happened to me. I believed in the way I taught children, valuing their autonomy and initiative. And I discovered I was teaching adults very differently, and that didn't seem right.

Further, I believed, as I still do, that decentering may be the most important outcome of studying human development. Decentering, learning that I am not the criterion for humanity. Traditional teaching, I realized, wasn't helping me to decenter; I taught well only those students who were most like me. And it wasn't helping my students to decenter; they didn't get to know enough about each other's lives.

What I've just said is a value judgment. All of us necessarily teach from our own values, and these are likely to be a complicated assortment of our views on the things that matter most. For example, while I believe that mature adults should strive to decenter, and that the study of development can contribute to this process, I also believe that the decision to study development should be an autonomous one, based on the individual's own wishes and desires.

Autonomy—self-centeredness—comes from decentering. (That's why I spent so much time on it in this class.) Before I can begin to understand and respect you, I must know and respect *me*.

Erikson has elaborated his earlier definition of autonomy (1950) with a description in which he emphasizes

This style of teaching is more work than traditional teaching, and it carries different rewards.

Decentering may be the most important outcome of studying human development.

Before I can begin to understand and respect you, I must know and respect me.

will. "Will is the unbroken determination to exercise free choice" (1978, p.30). Toddlers who exercise their will are not worrying about social constraints or the needs of others; they are trusting the adults to keep them safe. (A child who has not learned to trust is handicapped in developing autonomy; the world is too unsafe to take risks in.) The beautifully characteristic behavior of this age, in which the child alternates headlong dashes into the sunset with equally headlong returns to the safety of mommy's knees clutched tightly, dramatizes the dilemma which they continually face: "Wow!" vs. "Help!"

The adult has to decide whether to cultivate the will (by encouraging the "Wow!" the "I want," and the "No!" within the broadest possible range of safety and adult patience), or to break the will (by restraining and threatening the child, making it clear that her or his wishes do not come first in this world—instilling shame and doubt, in Erikson's words). This is an educational and childrearing issue many centuries old. "Breaking the will" was a clearly stated goal in Puritan America, and it remains a goal in many homes and schools, though perhaps it is no longer so confidently stated. The need for this decision reflects two sides of reality: the world *is* full of exciting challenges to be investigated, and the world *is* dangerous. We're back to the Elephant's Child, which I read at the last class. Which risk should we, as concerned adults, take?

Many adult students have lost most of their willfulness in the process of being socialized.

As a childrearer, I'm firmly on the side of cultivating the will, even though I don't always enjoy living with willful children. As a teacher of adults, I find that many of my students have lost most of their willfulness in the process of being socialized. They are polite, considerate, and obedient. They're nice people to have around. But many of them *don't know what they want.* They've been carefully taught in school that what they want doesn't matter; only what the teacher wants matters. Indeed, it is difficult to get as far as college without learning that.

Now, my first priority is that my students become competent, caring *wanters*—that they be able to make choices of what they want to do and learn. This is certainly not a first priority for all teachers, nor do I believe it should be. I taught 6- to 9-year-olds for several years recently, and for some of them I had quite different priorities, which I think are developmentally appropriate. [For one child, who was having trouble learning, my priority was still squarely in the area of autonomy; I wanted him to *want* something enough to work at it. It is only the children who are already accomplished wanters who are ready to be sat-upon in school for the sake of developing that side of their characters.]

Many teachers of adults have, appropriately, quite different priorities for their students. But this is mine. I am more concerned with motivation than with the content of learning. I want my students to have the experience of caring passionately about what they're doing in school. I want them to learn, as prospective teachers, that school is a place where it is possible and desirable to care about one's learning. I think caring leads to quality learning, to persistence in the face of obstacles, to a joyful view of what teaching and learning can be like. Of course, learning is not all joyful. But some of it is, and I want them to know that.

The devisers of behavioral objectives are uninclined to value the will. Their interest is in impersonal, dispassionate, measurable outcomes, and so their objectives are frequently stated in such terms as "The student will ..." or "Eighty percent of the students will ..." (and what happens to the rest of them?). Objectives of this sort permit the student no autonomy. Nor is the teacher in control of what "the student will," despite the confident phrasing; it is entirely possible that the student will not. Hence that 20% margin for error—an arbitrary figure if there ever was one.

I find it both more accurate and more appropriate to say, "*I* will...." I do have control over my own behavior,

> The devisers of behavioral objectives are uninclined to value the will.

113

*Caring leads to qual-
ity learning, to per-
sistence in the face
of obstacles, to a
joyful view of what
teaching and learn-
ing can be like.*

Subjects & Predicates

and, in exerting it, I am being autonomous. As teacher I
will engage in these kinds of behavior, and I will be accountable for what *I* do. I will ask my students to be
accountable for what *they* do; they are adults, and I choose
to treat them that way. In behavioral terms, my responsibility to them is to reinforce their wishes and desires.

Child development, human development, begins with
the *achievement* of humanity, in Bettelheim's words (1967).
The young child must learn to act

> ... in a way that affects the world around him, learn
> there is a self and non-self, and learn that he can

114

influence the non-self in an understandable cause-and-effect manner. In his own terms, Bettelheim is talking about the exercise of power as a condition for self-esteem and full humanity. (Ryan, 1976, pp. 159–160)

Children and adults who get stuck in this process fall short of full humanity and may never achieve it in their lifetimes. They become victims, unable to exert power on their own behalf. Schools, together with other social institutions, create many victims. There is no neutral education; education either domesticates or liberates. The human being's vocation is to be *more*, to grow in effectiveness in critical thinking and actions (Freire, 1970). I want to empower students, whoever they are.

Education either domesticates or liberates.

In doing so, I am not only reinforcing their overt wishes and desires, I am also challenging them. Not all students want to be empowered; a passive role is familiar and comfortable. "Teaching is not pleasing people. It is opening them to possibilities" (Stine in Jones, 1983, p. 89).

I find I must keep asking myself: Am I teaching to the uniqueness of students, to help them be more fully who they are? Or am I teaching to standardize, to sort and classify students, to fit them for defined niches in society? In Grace Rotzel's words:

> There are two views of education: one, that a man should be educated to be what he is, and the other, to be what he is not. The first retains man's idiosyncrasies, the second tries to eradicate all those that do not conform to the mores of the society of which he is a part. (1971, p. 92)

I think both views are necessary. The first is concerned with education, in the root sense of the word, *educere*, to lead out. The second is concerned with socialization, with learning to function smoothly in a social group. I'm in favor of alternatives, and choices among them, for both teachers and learners. At any one time, I think a teacher has to take her stand, to decide where her lot is cast; she can't be all things to all people. Later, she may decide to change, but what does she stand for now?

Right now, I'm firmly committed to the leading-out function of teaching. I enjoy teaching this way; it fits my temperament. I never know just what will happen next, and that's exciting, whereas just covering content I already know would be a bore. I think more people ought to be teaching this way, because the balance leans heavily in the other direction. Higher education offers students more opportunities for fitting-into-slots than it does opportunities for uniqueness. This is a pity, I think, if for no other reason than boredom, which affects both teachers and learners.

> I think the most dangerous thing that is happening to children in this country is boredom. This is more dangerous than any of the other things that are happening (and there are plenty of other dangerous things). But the transcendent boredom—to be shut up in a room, away from anything that moves or breathes or grows, in a controlled temperature, hour after hour— means that we are taking away from them any kind of chance of responsiveness. (Mead, 1973, p. 329)

By the time these children get to college they're so used to being bored in school that they take boredom for granted as the way things are supposed to be. (And when they go home they turn on the TV, since they have never learned active ways of making life interesting for themselves.) I think they're long overdue for a chance to play, to discover the delights of diversity and the unexpected, to find out who they and those other people really are, and what turns them on. I get scared by many of the highs that these bored kids and the adults they become find for themselves; I think they're dead ends, sometimes literally. Learning is for me a natural high. I believe it can be for many people, and I'd like to turn some of them on.

Many teachers who start out with this inspirational view of teaching quickly get disillusioned. They care passion-

Higher education offers students more opportunities for fitting-into-slots than it does opportunities for uniqueness.

ately about what they're teaching, but they find that their students don't. There is a book about the first-year experiences of six high school teachers (Ryan, 1970) which saddens me because, of the six, only one really begins his teaching by paying attention to who the students are. All the rest get stuck in power trips and anxieties about discipline and covering the course content.

In my experience you have to begin by finding out what the students care passionately, or even moderately, about, and then build bridges. We're back to respecting the idiosyncrasies of individual learners and nurturing them and helping them grow. The assumption that well-planned, well-presented content yields learning is simplistic, as the normal grade curve reflects. Actually, the degree to which the grade curve is taken for granted makes it clear that this assumption is not widely held. Instead it is assumed that the teacher's responsibility ends with the imparting of the information, and it's the students' responsibility whether they learn it or not.

I see this as an elitist view of education. It's one I used to hold but have since rejected. In this view, schools are for the good students—the ones who learn when they are taught, who fit the system as it exists. Schools are designed to preserve and foster this elite in order to maintain academic standards of excellence. In schools everyone but the good students falls short.

The alternative view is that everyone can and is entitled to learn. A student having difficulties with the system is entitled to have changes made in that system (Ryan, 1976, p. 263).

Both these views are extreme. No teacher will meet the needs of all her students and she shouldn't wallow in guilt over it. But every student deserves a chance, somewhere, some time, to thrive as a learner. I give up on a few of my students; they seem to me to be in the wrong place at the wrong time. Some colleges have many more such students. School, or this school, or my class isn't a good fit for them; they should be somewhere else. But there

You begin by finding out what the students care passionately about, and then build bridges.

Everyone can, and is entitled to, learn.

117

are other nonthrivers with whom I expend a great deal of energy trying to find the "hook," in David Hawkins's words, on which they can be caught—the point of encounter with a learning task at which they will discover themselves to be both motivated and competent. I think it's worth the effort.

> I believe that education should produce competence in making choices and commitment to one's choices. Individuals differ widely in learning style, ability, achievement and interests. They learn in their own sequence and on their own time schedule. Learners should have the time and resources to immerse themselves fully in what interests them *now*. This is crucial to the development of commitment, self-confidence, and attention.
>
> Intellectual development is more than anything else a matter of intense curiosity and problem-solving. In an era of rapid social change, intelligence becomes functional; someone has to ask the important questions and keep looking for new solutions. My concern for contemporary education is that it produce intelligence and commitment. (Jones, 1973, p. 43)

Intellectual development is more a matter of intense curiosity and problem-solving.

To accomplish this goal, I think radical changes are in order—not necessarily in the whole educational system, but in many little pockets. But why would any of us want to change things? As teachers, we are members of the elite group that the system is dedicated to preserving. Change is risky and uncomfortable; adventures are not all pony rides in May sunshine (Tolkien, 1937). Known evils are safer than those which we, like Hamlet, know not of.

I don't have any illusions about changing higher education. It has a long tradition, and traditions have much to recommend them. They are worth following unless you have clear gut-level feelings that something isn't working for you—that you're selling out your values. If you feel, strongly, that your students have unmet needs, or that you do, then you may be ready to invest the energy and take the risks that change making involves. The rewards, I find, more than compensate for those I got by being the star of the show. I'm not just the teacher, running through all this familiar material again; I'm an active learner along with the students. I learn a great deal about individuals and their differences, which contributes to my decentering process. And I get to orchestrate a group process, to put people in touch with each other, to build a network of friends and fellow learners. Giving up the star role, I get relationships instead. One of my graduate students, team-teaching with me and reading students' folders, exclaimed, "This is so much fun!" She went on, "Being on the other side is fascinating. I've always valued writing as a student; now I see how important it is to the teacher. You get to know students much better than the teacher of adults ordinarily does" (Carol Bowman, personal communication).

A preschool teacher might say the same thing, comparing herself to an elementary teacher. Sitting on the floor and observing, rather than standing up there in front of the class and talking, she really gets to know children. That's where I'm coming from. I never would have been a teacher if I hadn't discovered preschool.

This kind of learning experience *matters* to people. The last class session is often incredibly moving, as people share their feelings about their learning and about each other. It's altogether different from ending with a final exam. This ending is more like a beginning, full of questions rather than answers—questions to keep wondering about, and some people to keep in touch with so we can keep wondering together. *A Sense of Wonder*, Rachel Carson (1956) called her book about exploring the natural world with children. I feel the same way about exploring human development with adults—the wonder of it!

To make effective change in educational settings, you can't, of course, just talk about how good what you're doing makes you feel. Schools pride themselves on being rational, so you need a rationale—a set of logical argu-

My concern for contemporary education is that it produce intelligence and commitment.

ments, quoting suitable authorities, to justify what you're doing. And you need a model, someone who's been there before and can suggest useful organizational and survival strategies. There are not many models for open-structure teaching of adults, though there are a good many for open-structure teaching of young children.

So that's what this book is for. I have tried to describe the kinds of things that can go on in this sort of classroom for adults just in case you're one of those few teachers who might want to try it.

18

Postscript: What If?

So I think a class of 35 is large, and I have couches in my classroom, and I don't have to grade or follow someone else's course outline? You never had it so good.

What if . . .

. . . I had 50 or more students in a class—or hundreds, even?

Steve Monk teaches math at the University of Washington to very large classes. He uses an active-learning approach, working with his teaching assistants (Finkel & Monk, 1978). His book offers a rationale and a procedure for designing learning activities; it also has a lot to say about the joys and challenges of getting off of center stage.

Sharon Stine has written about teaching classes of nearly 100 (Jones, 1983, p. 70). She used circulating class books, with a page (or several pages) for each student's writing, rather than folders. In a large class, weekly reading of students' writing becomes unwieldy for the teacher. It is possible, however, for students to read and respond to each other's writing, given in-class time and clear guidelines. Writing needs response; it doesn't all have to be teacher response.

. . . I had to write behavioral objectives?

I'd fake them; that's easy to do. I'd state them as broadly as I could get away with. Most places just require the written objectives; they don't require proof that students have achieved them. As I've explained, I have gross behavioral objectives for my students, but they're things I want students to do all along the way, not end measures of achievement.

. . . I had to grade?

I still wouldn't use exams; they get in the way of the process. As a visiting instructor at the University of Alaska, I've had to grade; I used a simple contract system, with students choosing their grade based on quantity of written work. (I can return papers for further work if I have questions about their quality.) Stephanie Feeney and Sharon Stine, who have had to give grades in their university classes, have each written about the process in *On the Growing Edge* (Jones, 1983). I respect their solutions.

. . . I had to schedule a final exam?

I'd schedule it. But an exam can be many things. It can be a self- and peer-evaluation process like that which I used in this class. I want the ending of a class to be friendly, not formidable.

. . . my class met for 50 minutes every Monday, Wednesday, and Friday?

That's harder. I'd divide everything into smaller pieces, and I'd try to get the class rescheduled or offer to teach the evening section instead.

. . . I taught in an open-admission, lower-division program and my students weren't very literate or motivated to learn?

I always have a few students who aren't very literate. I try to respond to their writing with the same respect for whatever they have to say that I give the highly articulate. JoeAnn Dugger and Adele Hanson have had experience teaching whole classes of such students; their somewhat divergent reactions appear in *On the Growing Edge.* Ira Shor (1980) has written a compelling book on this issue describing his active-learning, empowering approaches in community college English classes.

. . . I had to teach in an altogether hard, inflexible environment—an amphitheater, say, or a foods lab with immovable tables?

Real people write and do research.

I'd complain. I'd move outdoors whenever possible. (See Greenleaf in Jones, 1983, for some possible consequences.) I'd move everything movable in the room and encourage students to think about learning environments and be critical and creative.

. . . I didn't have all these graduate students and their writing and research projects to quote from?

I'd use (as I do) whatever personal experiences I have—stories about children I've taught, stories about my own children, stories other students and friends have told me. I haven't been quoting these people to brag about who I know, but simply to make the personal connection, to let students know that real people write and do research.

. . . I didn't know anything about the subject I was teaching?

I've had that experience. We began by sharing everyone's experiences on the topic, and we all kept reading. Friends have suggested that's the time you use a textbook, simply following it from week to week while you work to catch up on your knowledge. That's a useful strategy, too. However, it is a good learning experience, especially if you're a fairly experienced teacher, to tackle directly something new to you. Most teachers can teach better by getting in touch with and building on what they themselves really know, than by borrowing someone else's canned material and presenting it in a canned, half-understood fashion.

Most teachers can teach better by getting in touch with and building on what they themselves really know, than by borrowing someone else's canned material and presenting it in a canned, half-understood fashion.

> To the extent that a teacher is an artist, and according to Plato there should be no distinction, his inner eye has the native power, unatrophied, to hold the work he means to do. And in the places where he can't see, he has a trust in himself that he will see it, either in time for the occasion or eventually. And he would rather risk a blank in his teaching than expend cash on the middleman. (Ashton-Warner, 1964, p. 79)

. . . I were a new teacher and didn't have it all at my fingertips?

This was, in fact, my first child development class, but I've taught for many years, I know the subject well, and I can think on my feet. Two of my less-experienced friends, reading this manuscript, complained, "You have not written about the magical parts of your teaching. You make it sound so easy."

It isn't magic. Originally I put the pieces together intuitively, over a long period of experimentation, but at this point I know what they are, and I've tried to make them clear in this book. It's essential to build in a variety of getting-acquainted, networking activities: introductions, name tags, a class list, games, small-group discussions and tasks. It's important to be direct about my expectations, to give clear instructions about everything that is not a choice, and to give information about what's going to happen, even within the flexibility of an emergent curriculum—thus Things to Do, task instructions, the calendar. It's important that accountability be built in for both me and the students, that there be many opportunities for written feedback, that I pay attention to what's happening for each individual, and that self-evaluations be systematic and be shared with peers as well as with me. It's essential that direct connections be made between individuals' experience and the class content, that activities generate provocative questions and critical thinking about developmental issues. Essentially, the structure, not the content, comes first in planning. Given resources and a plan for interaction, content will emerge all over the place. Students *are* curious about child development; I want to tap that curiosity.

> The structure, not the content, comes first in planning.

Even if you do all these things, of course, that still won't get you through the actual doing of it. Nancy Jambor, as a new college teacher, has written:

> There are ways, subtle and obvious, in which the instructor needs to be seen as the authority. You have to be able to think on your feet, to answer challenges, to invent an activity or a meaning on the spot, to chor-

eograph interactions and to time events, to monitor the class and continually have a response for what happens next. (Jambor, personal communication)

Early in her class, Nancy found "a need from both sides—students and teacher—to keep a slight buffer zone or distance between us. That we are not peers is pretty evident in some respects. That they are used to such distance is very evident." But later, having gone through a period of some uneasiness, she wrote:

> The crisis seems to have crested and passed, and the distance is gone (except in a few instances, for brief moments)—cast off, I think. I know that I cast it off, and I think class members were just waiting for the high sign. It was necessary for me, for a while, to get my confidence up so that I could manage open classroom style. I am so glad I let go of the format I had been following; keeping my formal talking to a minimum is really much better. The tone in the room remains active and involved, instead of lapsing into morbundity because now, NOW, she will speak. In fact, for the project presentations today, we had some trouble getting people ready to listen. How ironic! How far we have come! (Jambor, personal communication)

In my experience, most students would really like classes to be more informal, relaxed, and personal, than they usually are. All of us, teachers and students, hide behind our tight little formalities, but being given permission not to is a real gift.

. . . you don't want to eliminate the distance between yourself and students? You don't want a class full of rampant feelings? You value the orderliness and predictability of traditional teaching, and you doubt your ability to handle all this unexpectedness and passion?

I'd go slow, looking at myself as a person, at my tolerance for ambiguity and my need to be perfect. To teach this way, you've got to be secure enough to be open and nondefensive. You've got to trust your students and be willing to give them personal support. And you need to

To teach this way, you've got to be secure enough to be open and nondefensive.

be nonjudgmental if you're going to ask people to take risks. Perfection is required of none of us; risk taking is. But if that's not where you are, let things be.

. . . you're not brave enough to make all these changes?

Don't. I didn't. This is how I teach now, but it happened over a good many years. Plan your class around lectures, if you will, but then throw in an activity from time to time and see what happens.

Nancy Jambor, teaching her first child development class, designed each 3-hour session as a combination of small-group interactions, lecture, and a film or time to "write/read/whatever." She "read a lot in order to prepare . . ." and by the fifth session she was beginning to wonder if the lectures

> . . . are getting in the way. Not that they aren't thoughtful or useful or helpful—I like them! But they dramatically change the tone of the class. They are the most distancing thing I do. I am wondering if they are not a vestigial limb of some sort—of my teaching anxieties (needing to be sure certain information goes out direct mail, needing to assert my knowledge) and their student anxieties (they all get into the taking-notes mode REAL fast when it's clear I am going to 'talk'). If I stopped preparing this hour's worth of talking, what would we do?
>
> A lecture is a pretty good disguise for information. When someone lectures, you know you are at the heart of the matter, right? How I would feel about dropping lectures is another matter. Partly, I would feel relieved. Partly, I would feel guilty; I am not "doing enough" for the class. Partly, I would feel that I was taking the class into uncharted waters. And then what? (Jambor, personal communication)

Once you start asking yourself how it might be different, change starts to creep in, risks and all.

Questions, questions. Once you start asking yourself how it might be different, change starts to creep in, risks and all.

If you have more "What ifs," write me at Pacific Oaks, 5 Westmoreland Place, Pasadena, CA 91103. I'll respond.

I may not have any good answers, but we can think about it together.

It's because I haven't had to fight a rigid system that I've been free to discover some of these approaches to teaching. But they *can* be applied elsewhere, as the teachers writing in *On the Growing Edge* (Jones, 1983) make clear.

Ashton-Warner, S. (1964). *Teacher.* New York: Bantam Books.

Bettelheim, B. (1967). *The empty fortress: Infantile autism and the growth of self.* New York: The Free Press.

Carson, R. (1956). *A sense of wonder.* New York: Harper & Row.

Dugger, J. (1983). The new kid on the block. In E. Jones (Ed.), *On the growing edge: Notes by college teachers making changes* (pp. 51–58). Pasadena: Pacific Oaks College.

Elkind, D. (1982, January). The hurried child. *Instructor, XCI,* 40–43.

Engelmann, S. (1971). Does the Piagetian approach imply instruction? In D. R. Green, M. P. Ford, & G. B. Flamer (Eds.), *Measurement and Piaget* (pp. 118–126). New York: McGraw-Hill.

Erikson, E. (1950). *Childhood and society.* New York: Norton.

Erikson, E. (Ed.). (1978). *Adulthood.* New York: Norton.

Feeney, S. (1983). Reflections on the grading process. In E. Jones (Ed.), *On the growing edge: Notes by college teachers making changes* (pp. 78–83). Pasadena: Pacific Oaks College.

Finkel, D., & Monk, S. (1978). *Contexts for learning: A teacher's guide to the design of intellectual experience.* Olympia, WA: The Evergreen State College.

Fraiberg, S. (1975). Intervention in infancy: A program for blind infants. In B. Z. Friedlander, G. M. Sterritt, & G. E. Kirk (Eds.), *Exceptional infant, vol. 3: Assessment and intervention* (pp. 40–62). New York: Brunner/Mazel.

Freire, P. (1970). *Pedagogy of the oppressed.* New York: Herder & Herder.

Gould, S. (1981). *The mismeasure of man.* New York: Norton.

Greenleaf, P. (1983). What can happen to you if you're not careful. In E. Jones (Ed.), *On the growing edge: Notes by college teachers making changes* (pp. 90–

92). Pasadena: Pacific Oaks College.

Hanson, A. (1983). Beginning where they are . . . and then what? In E. Jones (Ed.), *On the growing edge: Notes by college teachers making changes* (pp. 59–62). Pasadena: Pacific Oaks College.

Hawkins, D. (1970). Messing about in science. In *The ESS reader* (pp. 37–44). Newton, MA: Education Development Center.

Herndon, J. (1968). *The way it spozed to be.* New York: Simon & Schuster.

Jones, E. (1973). *Dimensions of teaching-learning environments.* Pasadena: Pacific Oaks College.

Jones, E. (Ed.). (1978). *Joys and risks in teaching young children.* Pasadena: Pacific Oaks College.

Jones, E. (Ed.). (1983). *On the growing edge: Notes by college teachers making changes.* Pasadena: Pacific Oaks College.

Katz, L. (1977). Challenges to early childhood educators. *Young Children, 32*(4), pp. 4–10.

Katz, L. (1975, March). Early childhood programs and ideological disputes. *The Educational Forum.* pp. 267–271.

Katz, L. (1980). Mothering and teaching: Some significant distinctions. In Lilian Katz et al. (Eds.), *Current topics in early childhood education* (Vol. 3). Norwood, NJ: Ablex.

Kipling, R. (1978). The elephant's child. In *Just so stories.* New York: Crown.

Kritchevsky, S., & Prescott, E. (1969). *Planning environments for young children.* Washington, DC: NAEYC.

Labinowicz, E. (1980). *The Piaget primer.* Menlo Park, CA: Addison-Wesley.

Maslow, A. (1962). *Toward a psychology of being.* New York: Van Nostrand Reinhold.

Mead, M. (1973). Can the socialization of children lead to greater acceptance of diversity? *Young Children, 28*(6), 322–329.

Orwell, G. (1981). *1984.* New York: Signet.

Piaget, J. (1973). *To understand is to invent.* New York: Grossman.

Prescott, E. (1973). *Who thrives in group day care?* Pasadena: Pacific Oaks College.

Rabiroff, B., & Prescott, E. (1978). The invisible child: Challenge to teacher attentiveness. In E. Jones (Ed.), *Joys and risks in teaching young children* (pp. 123–133). Pasadena: Pacific Oaks College.

Ramirez, M., & Castaneda, A. (1974). *Cultural democracy, bicognitive development and education.* New York: Academic Press.

Rodriguez, R. (1982). *Hunger of memory.* Boston: David Godine.

Rotzel, G. (1971). *The school in Rose Valley.* New York: Ballantine.

Ryan, K. (1970). *Don't smile until Christmas.* Chicago: University of Chicago.

Ryan, W. (1976). *Blaming the victim.* New York: Vintage.

Shor, I. (1980). *Critical teaching and everyday life.* Boston: South End Press.

Singer, D. (1972, June). Piglet, Pooh, and Piaget. *Psychology Today,* pp. 71–96.

Stine, S. (1983). Coping with the realities. In E. Jones (Ed.), *On the growing edge: Notes by college teachers making changes* (pp. 84–89). Pasadena: Pacific Oaks College.

Tolkien, J. R. R. (1937). *The Hobbit.* London: George Allen & Unwin.

Trook, E. (1983). Understanding teachers' use of power: A role playing activity. In E. Jones (Ed.), *On the growing edge: Notes by college teachers making changes* (pp. 15–22). Pasadena: Pacific Oaks College.

Tucker, S. (1978). *The earliest years* (filmstrip). Pasadena: Pacific Oaks College.

Weinstein, M., & Goodman, J. (1980). *Playfair.* San Luis Obispo, CA: Impact Publishers.

On Teaching Adults: Additional Reading

Baker, W. E., Leitman, A., Page, F., Sharkey, A., & Suhd, M. (1971). The creative environment workshop. *Young Children, 26*(4), 219–223.

Borton, T. (1970). *Reach, touch and teach.* New York: McGraw-Hill.

Brown, G. (1971). *Human teaching for human learning.* New York: Viking.

Gilstrap, R. L. (No date). Open education in the classroom: A professor's memo to his students. In *Winds of change: Teacher education for the open area school,* Bulletin ATE, 36.

Haglund, E. (1979, July). Building a learning environment: New directions in process teacher education. *Peabody Journal of Education,* pp. 288–293.

Heath, D. (1971). *Humanizing schools.* New York: Hayden.

Hoover, K. H. (1980). *College teaching today: A handbook for postsecondary instruction.* Boston: Allyn & Bacon.

Howe, L. W., & Howe, M. M. (1975). *Personalizing education: Values clarification and beyond.* New York: Hart.

Jones, E. (1980). Creating environments where teachers, like children, learn through play. *Child Care Information Exchange, 13,* pp. 1–5.

Jones, E. (1981). Open structures for adult learning: A theoretical base. *Educational Perspectives, 20,* pp. 4–7.

Jones, E. (1986). Perspectives on teacher education. Some relations between theory and practice. In L. Katz (Ed.), *Current topics in early childhood education* (vol. 6) (pp. 123–141). Norwood, NJ: Ablex.

Jones, E. (1979). Structuring environments for adult learning. In *Piagetian theory and its implications for the helping profession. Proceedings Eighth Interdisciplinary Conference* (Vol. 2) (pp. 295–300). Los Angeles: Univ. of Southern California.

Jones, E. (1978). Teacher education: Entertainment or interaction? *Young Children, 33*(3), 15–23.

Jones, E. (1981). Teacher education in action. In S. Kilmer (Ed.), *Advances in early education and day care* (Vol. 2) (pp. 91–127). Greenwich, CT: JAI Press.

Jones, E. (1984). Training individuals: In the classroom and out. In J. T. Greenman, & R. W. Fuqua (Eds.), *Making day care better: Training, evaluation and the process of change* (pp. 185–201). New York: Teachers College.

Kelley, E. (1951). *The workshop way of learning.* New York: Harper & Bros.

Knowles, M. (1978). *The adult learner: A neglected species.* Houston: Gulf.

Lyon, H. C. (1971). *Learning to feel, feeling to learn.* Columbus: Merrill.

Macrorie, K. (1970). *Uptaught.* New York: Hayden.

Macrorie, K. (1974). *A vulnerable teacher.* New York: Hayden.

Marshall, S. (1968). *Adventure in creative education.* New York: Pergamon.

McKeachie, W. J. (1973). *Teaching tips: A guidebook for the beginning college teacher.* Lexington, MA: Heath.

McVickar, P. (1981). *Imagination: Key to human potential.* Pasadena: Pacific Oaks College.

Miller, J. P. (1976). *Humanizing the classroom: Models of teaching in affective education.* New York: Praeger.

Rogers, C. (1969). *Freedom to learn.* Columbus: Merrill.

Simpson, E. L. (1976). *Humanistic education.* Cambridge, MA: Ballinger.

Wasserman, S. (1973, March). The open classroom in teacher education, or putting your money where your mouth is. *Childhood Education,* pp. 295–301.

Weber, S., & Somers, B. J. (No date). Humanistic education at the college level: A new strategy and some techniques. Unpublished manuscript. Available from B. Somers, Professor of Psychology, California State University at Los Angeles, 5151 State University Dr., Los Angeles, CA 90032.

Wolman, M. (1969). Training Head Start teachers in Alaska. *Educational Leadership, 26*(6), 603–609.

Some Sources of Activities

for getting acquainted with yourself and others, change of pace, movement and laughter, and learning by doing

(All these sources have suggestions useful for teachers of adults. Some are directed to teachers of children and could be used at either level.)

Bartal, L., & Ne'eman, N. (1975). *Movement awareness and creativity.* New York: Harper & Row.

Canfield, J., & Wells, H. C. (1976). *100 ways to enhance self-concept in the classroom.* Englewood Cliffs, NJ: Prentice-Hall.

Castillo, G. (1974). *Left-handed teaching.* New York: Praeger.

Curwin, R. L., & Curwin, G. (1974). *Developing individual values in the classroom.* Palo Alto: Learning handbooks.

Curwin, R. L., & Fuhrmann, B. (1975). *Discovering your teaching self.* Englewood Cliffs, NJ: Prentice-Hall.

DeMille, R. (1973). *Put your mother on the ceiling.* New York: Viking.

Fluegelman, A. (Ed.). (1976). *The new games book.* Garden City, NJ: Doubleday.

Fluegelman, A. (Ed.). (1981). *More new games!* Garden City, NJ: Doubleday.

Greer, M., & Rubinstein, B. (1972). *Will the real teacher please stand up?* Pacific Palisades, CA: Goodyear.

Harmin, M., & Gregory, T. (1974). *Teaching is . . . .* Chicago: Science Research Associates.

Harmin, M., & Sax, S. (1977). *A peaceable classroom.* New York: Winston.

Hawley, R. C. (1975). *Value exploration through role playing.* New York: Hart.

Hendricks, G., & Wills, R. (1975). *The centering book*. Englewood Cliffs, NJ: Prentice-Hall.

Hendricks, G., Wills, R., & Roberts, T. B. (1977). *The second centering book*. Englewood Cliffs, NJ: Prentice-Hall.

Michaelis, B., & Michaelis, D. (1977). *Learning through noncompetitive activities and play*. Palo Alto, CA: Learning handbooks.

Orlick, T. (1978). *The cooperative sports and games book*. New York: Pantheon.

Rozman, D. (1976). *Meditation for children*. Millbrae, CA: Celestial Arts.

Schranck, J. (1972). *Teaching human beings*. Boston: Beacon Press.

Timmerman, T., & Ballard, J. (1975). *Stategies in humanistic education* (Vol. 1). Amherst, MA: Mandala.

Weitz, D. (1974). *Eggs and peanut butter*. Menlo Park, CA: Word Wheel Press.

Appendix

Resource
Materials

Getting Acquainted

1. On a small piece of paper, write:
   a. the names of three children you know or have known (first name only)
   b. the age of each child (now or when you knew her or him)
   c. two descriptive words for each child:
      1) something you like(d) about her or him
      2) something you don't like about her or him.
2. Pin your paper on yourself—back or front.
3. Walk around the room, reading other people's papers.
4. When you find one that particularly interests you, ask that person to sit down with you and tell you about *one* of her or his children (save the others). In turn, tell her or him about one of yours.
5. Ask another pair of people to make a foursome with you. In turn, tell the group about another one of your children—one you haven't talked about yet.
6. Help each other to find:
   a. Things To Do (take one)
   b. the reading list (take one)
   c. Child Development: Some Basic Assumptions (take one)
   d. the Calendar (Find the snacks column. Sign up to bring snacks once every 3 weeks during the semester.)
   e. the box of folders (Take a blank one and put your name, address, and phone number on it. We'll make a class list from it.)
7. Write: a. three things you already know about child development.
   b. one question you'd like to discuss in class.
   Put your writing in your folder.
8. At about 2:15, we will have a class meeting. If you finish writing before then, look over the Reading List and mark for yourself:
   any books you've already read
   any books you'd particularly like to read.

9. Do any self-preservation activities (go to the bathroom, eat, drink, wiggle) before the class meeting.

(In this class we will sometimes have a break and sometimes not, but there will always be changes of activities. It's up to you to take care of your personal needs, and it is generally OK to leave a discussion for that purpose.)

Things To Do

1. *Talk* and *listen* in class. Get acquainted with other class members as resources for your learning. Contribute from your experience to their learning.

2. *Read*: Two or more books chosen from the Reading List (or other sources).

Handouts provided in class.

Notes to you in your folder.

3. *Observe* children's and adults' behavior. Observation instructions will be given in class.

4. *Write*: In response to questions raised in class.

In response to your reading.

In response to your observations.

5. *Evaluate* what you've done and what you've learned, in mid-semester and at the end of the class. Your final evaluation is due in writing at the next-to-last session and will be shared orally in class at the last session. Ask yourself these questions and write your answers:

a. What did you do for this class?

(Be specific: attendance, discussion participation, observing, reading, teaching, writing, conversations)

b. What didn't you do that you wish you had done? Why?

c. Of all the things you did, what did you learn most from and/or enjoy most? What were you most resentful of or frustrated or bored by? Explain why.

d. How did the class structure work for you? What was there too much of? Too little of? (for example, group discussions, lectures, films, writing, choices, reading, directions, theories) What did you need from the instructor that you did/didn't get?

Child Development: Some Basic Assumptions

1. There are basic needs common to all human beings.

2. Development—physical, social, emotional, intellectual—occurs in stages and in a predictable sequence.

3. Children are not all alike. Normal development includes broad individual variations.

4. Children have a perspective all their own; they see and understand the world differently than adults. Therefore, to understand children and their behavior, you must observe them, take them seriously, and try to put yourself in their shoes.

5. Children learn through play.

6. Children are dependent on adults. To understand them, we need to know something about the personal, social, and cultural characteristics of the adults in their lives.

7. Child behavior can be explained from a variety of theoretical frameworks. All of us build and use theories all the time in order to understand our experiences. It is important to identify the theories we use, to know what our assumptions and values are.

Before Birth

Before a child is born, there are value choices to be made. Here are some dilemmas for your group to discuss. You have an hour. Follow this procedure:

a. The group member with the earliest birthday in the year reads #1 aloud. Each of you check the choice that is your first, impulsive reaction. Then discuss your choices. Ask each other questions and argue your point of view, but be respectful of others' points of view. Feel free to make up additional details about the people in the story.

Can your group come to agreement about the best choice? Or do you have different values which make that impossible?

b. Repeat this process for #2 through #5, taking turns in order of your birthdays. The person with the last birthday is also timekeeper; allow about 10 minutes on each question.

c. We'll come back to compare notes in the large group at 3:45.

Dilemmas

1. Terry is 15 and has just discovered she is pregnant by her boyfriend, Joe. Should she: _____ marry Joe, _____ have an abortion, _____ have the child and give it up for adoption, _____ keep the child and continue to live with her parents, _____ other (what?).

2. Pearl and Merle are both 18, have been married for 6 months and are living with her parents. Both have minimum-wage jobs and plan to move into their own apartment soon. Now Pearl is pregnant. Should they: _____ have an abortion, _____ put the infant in child care so Pearl can keep working, _____ stay with her parents so she can stay home with the baby, _____ other (what?).

3. Rachel and Rupert are 31 and 28 and have been married for 6 months. Both have professional jobs and they live in an adults-only apartment. They have just found a house they want to buy; the payments will take one full salary. Now Rachel is pregnant. Should they: _____ have an abortion and buy the house, _____ put the infant in a child care center so Rachel can keep working and they can buy the house, _____ find an apartment which takes children so Rachel can stay home with the baby, _____ find an apartment which takes children so Rupert can stay home with the baby, _____ other (what?).

4. Jane is 35 and she and Dick (age 37) enjoy their four children very much. She is pregnant again, and amniocentesis* shows that the baby has Down Syndrome and will be handicapped. Should they: _____ have an abortion, _____ have the child, raise him, and plan to care

---

*a medical procedure in which amniotic fluid is withdrawn from the womb to check for genetic defects in the fetus. It also reveals the sex of the unborn child.

for him for the rest of their lives, _____ have the child and plan to institutionalize him, _____ other (what?).

5. Janet is 37 and pregnant for the first time. Amniocentesis shows that the baby has Down Syndrome. Should she and Mark (age 45): _____ have an abortion, _____ have the child, raise her, and plan to care for her for the rest of their lives, _____ have the child, plan to institutionalize her, and have another child as soon as possible, _____ other (what?).

Understanding Teachers' Use of Power: A Role-Playing Activity

Eve Trook

Power ON, power WITH, and power FOR

Those of us who wish to be nonoppressive teachers of young children have rejected the autocractic expertise of the teacher model most of us experienced in childhood, but we are not, if we are thoughtful, likely to be comfortable with the image of preschool children doing their own thing. We know from experience that we control the language and thinking of young children, shape their values, and generally pattern their responses to life, because we have immense amounts of power while they have only small fragments. We seek to devise a teacher model that will allow us to free children from our power without abdicating it, so that they will have the opportunity to create their own humanity.

The model on which this role play is based includes these assumptions:

1. If we become consciously aware of our power, we can use it intentionally.

2. Power is not finite. My process of power acquisition does not diminish anyone else's power, nor is it beyond the grasp of children.

3. If we accept our power in order to create more power, for ourselves and with children, we can become responsible but nonoppressive teachers.

4. To maintain a nonoppressive process, we need peer support. Only from our peers, those equal in power and

possessing knowledge of the uniqueness of our lives, can we acquire sufficiently detailed judgments to aid us in this process. There are no lists of oppressive and liberating teacher behaviors. Judgments rest on the relationship of the individuals involved in each unique interaction, both affective and cognitive.

5. Those rare, mutually creative interactions which are the high point of our human existence are possible only with peers. Thus it is clear that our liberation is directly related to our ability to be liberators, i.e., to help others, including children, create the power that makes them our peers as often as possible.

Power exercised *ON* a child means that the child has no real choice, i.e., the child is *oppressed.*

Power exercised *FOR* a child means that the child is provided experiences that contribute to the development of self-esteem and confidence that lead to power for the child, i.e., the child is *facilitated.*

Power exercised *WITH* a child means that teacher and child are equals learning together, and the child acquires new power, i.e., the child and teacher are *liberated.*

The critical difference between FOR and WITH is teacher control. Power used FOR the child means the teacher is intentionally guiding, structuring, or supporting the child toward a goal. Power WITH the child means both teacher and child share a sense of wonder and are creating together.

Judging

The judges must provide the teacher with feedback as to whether power was created for the teacher and/or the child. The following is a suggested model for the evaluation procedure.

1. The chief judge asks the child whether power was exercised *ON, FOR,* or *WITH* her or him.

2. The chief judge asks the other judges to state individually their judgments as to whether teacher power was used *ON, FOR,* or *WITH* the child. The chief judge

is responsible for keeping judges on the subject. There is a tendency for judges to explore issues and refer to the frustrations of their own teaching experiences rather than making a judgment about the unique individual experience they have just observed. Judges must provide teachers with feedback as to exactly how they oppressed, facilitated, or liberated. Teachers should persistently ask judges for this information or the simulation will be of little value to them.

3. If the child and the judges feel that there existed during the role playing more than one incident to evaluate (e.g., one liberating, one oppressive), then the judges decide, after enumerating the incidents, the overall character of the role-playing period.

4. Power ON and WITH in extreme cases will be fairly easy to judge. The difficulty will be the tendency of the judges to give the teacher the benefit of the doubt and judge FOR over ON. If there is doubt, and if we want to create power for children, we must be willing to take responsibility for our power and see oppression when it is there.

5. Be especially wary of teachers who praise children and thereby oppress them. We do not presume to praise equals, although we might specifically appreciate in detail a thing they do well.

6. If a child feels oppressed, then she or he is judged to be oppressed. If a child does not feel oppressed, but the judges feel the child was oppressed and can gain the child's agreement, the child is judged oppressed.

Severely critical analyses of oppression are necessary to enable liberation of children. Because most of us deny oppression to ourselves, we must seriously consider the validity of even the faintest feelings of oppression which any player might be sensitive to. If a child claims not to have been oppressed, but a judge feels that she or he was, that judge must make her or his feelings as explicit as possible so that the truth of the oppression, if it in fact existed, becomes undeniable.

I. Your parents' view

What kind of person did your parents want you to become? Check each of the characteristics which they felt were generally desirable and should be encouraged. Then double-check the five characteristics which they considered most important, to be encouraged above all others. Draw a line through those characteristics which they considered undesirable and usually discouraged or punished. (If your parents were not in agreement, mark for either one or for both separately.)

W hat Is an Ideal Child?

_____ Adventurous
_____ Affectionate
_____ A good guesser
_____ Altruistic
_____ Always asking questions
_____ Athletic
_____ Attempts difficult jobs
_____ A self-starter
_____ Becomes preoccupied with tasks
_____ Careful
_____ Cautious
_____ Competitive
_____ Completes work on time
_____ Conforming
_____ Considerate of others
_____ Cooperative
_____ Courageous
_____ Courteous
_____ Creative
_____ Critical of others
_____ Curious
_____ Desires to excel
_____ Determined
_____ Domineering
_____ Emotional

_____ Energetic
_____ Fault finding
_____ Fearful
_____ Friendly
_____ Gets good grades
_____ Healthy
_____ Independent in judgment
_____ Industrious
_____ Intelligent
_____ Intuitive
_____ Likes to work alone
_____ Likes school
_____ Never bored
_____ Negativistic
_____ Obedient
_____ Persistent
_____ Physically attractive
_____ Physically strong
_____ Proud
_____ Quiet
_____ Rebellious
_____ Receptive to ideas of others
_____ Refined
_____ Regresses occasionally (playful, childish)
_____ Remembers well

_____ Self-assertive
_____ Self-confident
_____ Self-satisfied
_____ Self-sufficient
_____ Sense of beauty
_____ Sense of humor
_____ Sensitive
_____ Sincere
_____ Socially well adjusted
_____ Spirited in disagree-
ment
_____ Strives for distant
goals

_____ Stubborn
_____ Talkative
_____ Thorough
_____ Timid
_____ Unwilling to accept
things on others' say-
so
_____ Versatile
_____ Visionary
_____ Willing to accept
judgments of authori-
ties
_____ Willing to take risks

II. Your own view

What kind of person would you like your child to become? Check each of the characteristics which you feel
is generally desirable and should be encouraged. Then
double-check the five characteristics which you consider
most important, to be encouraged above all others. Draw
a line through those characteristics which you consider
undesirable and would usually discourage or punish.

_____ Adventurous
_____ Affectionate
_____ A good guesser
_____ Altruistic
_____ Always asking ques-
tions
_____ Athletic
_____ Attempts difficult jobs
_____ A self-starter
_____ Becomes preoccu-
pied with tasks
_____ Careful
_____ Cautious
_____ Competitive
_____ Completes work on
time

_____ Conforming
_____ Considerate of others
_____ Cooperative
_____ Courageous
_____ Courteous
_____ Creative
_____ Critical of others
_____ Curious
_____ Desires to excel
_____ Determined
_____ Domineering
_____ Emotional
_____ Energetic
_____ Fault finding
_____ Fearful
_____ Friendly

_____ Gets good grades
_____ Healthy
_____ Independent in judgment
_____ Industrious
_____ Intelligent
_____ Intuitive
_____ Likes to work alone
_____ Likes school
_____ Never bored
_____ Negativistic
_____ Obedient
_____ Persistent
_____ Physically attractive
_____ Physically strong
_____ Proud
_____ Quiet
_____ Rebellious
_____ Receptive to ideas of others
_____ Refined
_____ Regresses occasionally (playful, childish)
_____ Remembers well
_____ Self-assertive

_____ Self-confident
_____ Self-satisfied
_____ Self-sufficient
_____ Sense of beauty
_____ Sense of humor
_____ Sensitive
_____ Sincere
_____ Socially well adjusted
_____ Spirited in disagreement
_____ Strives for distant goals
_____ Stubborn
_____ Talkative
_____ Thorough
_____ Timid
_____ Unwilling to accept things on others' say-so
_____ Versatile
_____ Visionary
_____ Willing to accept judgments of authorities
_____ Willing to take risks

R eading List

Observations of children (and some theory based on them)

Barker, R. (1951). *One boy's day.* New York: Harper Bros.

Brazelton, T. B. (1969). *Infants and mothers: Differences in development.* New York: Delacorte.

Brazelton, T. B. (1974). *Toddlers and parents: A declaration of independence.* New York: Delacorte.

Brody, S. (1978). *Mothers, fathers and children: Explorations in the formation of character in the first seven years.* New York: International Universities Press.

Brody, S. (1956). *Patterns of mothering.* New York: International Universities Press.

Church, J. (Ed.). (1966). *Three babies: Biographies of cognitive development.* New York: Random House.

Coles, R. (1967). *Children of crisis I. A study of courage and fear.* Boston: Little, Brown.

Coles, R. (1971). *Children of crisis II. Migrants, sharecroppers, mountaineers.* Boston: Little, Brown.

Coles, R. (1971). *Children of crisis III. The South goes North.* Boston: Little, Brown.

Coles, R. (1977). *Children of crisis IV. Eskimos, Chicanos, Indians.* Boston: Little, Brown.

Coles, R. (1977). *Children of crisis V. Privileged ones: The well-off and the rich in America.* Boston: Little, Brown.

Elkind, D. (1974). *Children and adolescents: Interpretive essays on Jean Piaget.* New York: Oxford.

Erikson, E. H. (1950). *Childhood and society.* New York: Norton.

Escalona, S. K. (1968). *The roots of individuality: Normal patterns of development in infancy.* Chicago: Aldine.

Fraiberg, S. (1959). *The magic years.* New York: Norton.

Lewis, C. (1946). *Children of the Cumberland.* New York: Columbia University.

Murphy, L. B. (1956). *Personality in young children: Colin—a normal child* (Vol. 2). New York: Basic Books.

Murphy, L. B. (1962). *The widening world of childhood:*

Paths toward mastery. New York: Basic Books.

Piaget, J. (1954). *The construction of reality in the child.* New York: Basic Books.

Piaget, J. (1955). *The language and thought of the child.* New York: New American Library.

Senn, M. J. E., & Hartford, C. (Eds.). (1968). *The firstborn: Experiences of eight American families.* Cambridge: Harvard University Press.

Thomas, A., Chess, S., & Birch, H. (1968). *Temperament and behavior disorders in children.* New York: New York University Press.

Observations of children in schools and preschools

Ashton-Warner, S. (1963). *Teacher.* New York: Simon & Schuster.

Dennison, G. (1969). *The lives of children: The story of the first street school.* New York: Random House.

Hawkins, F. (1974). *The logic of action: Young children at work.* New York: Pantheon.

Kohl, H. (1968). *Thirty-six children.* New York: Signet.

O'Gorman, N. (1970). *The storefront: A community of children on 129th Street and Madison Avenue.* New York: Harper & Row.

Schulman, A. S. (1967). *Absorbed in living, children learn.* Washington, DC: NAEYC.

Woodcock, L. P. (1941). *Life and ways of the two-year-old.* New York: E. P. Dutton.

Observations of children with special needs (and some therapeutic interventions)

Axline, V. (1964). *Dibs: In search of self.* Boston: Houghton Mifflin.

Baruch, D. (1952). *One little boy.* New York: Julian.

Bettelheim, B. (1967). *The empty fortress: Infantile autism and the birth of self.* Glencoe, IL: Free Press.

Bettelheim, B. (1950). *Love is not enough.* Glencoe, IL: The Free Press.

Greenfeld, J. (1972). *A child called Noah: A family journal.* New York: Warner.

Hawkins, F. (1974). *The logic of action.* New York: Pantheon.

Kaufman, B. (1976). *Son-Rise.* New York: Warner.

MacCracken, M. (1973). *A circle of children.* Philadelphia: Lippincott.

MacCracken, M. (1981). *City Kid.* Boston: Little, Brown.

MacCracken, M. (1976). *Lovey: A very special child.* Philadelphia: Lippincott.

Fiction and biography

Angelou, M. (1970). *I know why the caged bird sings.* New York: Random House.

Bradbury, R. (1957). *Dandelion wine.* New York: Bantam Books.

Cozzens, J. G. (1964). *Children and others.* New York: Harcourt Brace.

Ewald, C. (1962). *My little boy.* New York: Horizon Press.

Godden, R. (1981). *The battle of the Villa Fiorita.* New York: Harper & Row.

Golding, W. (1954). *Lord of the flies.* New York: Putnam.

Goudge, E. (1979). *The rosemary tree.* New York: Buccaneer Books.

Jackson, S. (1953). *Life among the savages.* New York: Farrar, Strauss & Young.

Jackson, S. (1975). *Raising demons.* New York: Popular Library.

Lee, H. (1960). *To kill a mockingbird.* Philadelphia: Lippincott.

Parks, G. (1963). *The learning tree.* New York: Fawcett.

Potok, C. (1975). *The beginning.* New York: Knopf.

Potok, C. (1972). *My name is Asher Lev.* New York: Knopf.

Wright, R. (1945). *Black boy.* New York: Harper & Row.

Stories for children about children

Burnett, F. (1911). *The secret garden.* Philadelphia: Lippincott.

Clemens, S. (Mark Twain). (1979). *The adventures of Tom Sawyer.* New York: Dodd Mead.

Dodgson, C. (Lewis Carroll). (1979). *Alice's adventures*

in Wonderland. New York: Grosset & Dunlap.

Fitzhugh, L. (1964). *Harriet the spy*. New York: Harper & Row.

Godden, R. (1972). *The Diddakoi*. New York: Viking.

Goudge, E. (1978). *Linnets and Valerians*. New York: Avon Books.

Goudge, E. (1978). *The little white horse*. New York: Avon Books.

Milne, A. A. (1926). *Winnie the Pooh*. New York: Dutton.

Milne, A. A. (1928). *The house at Pooh Corner*. New York: Dutton.

O'Hara, M. (1941). *My friend Flicka*. Philadelphia: Lippincott.

Paterson, K. (1977). *Bridge to Terabithia*. New York: Crowell.

Rawlings, M. K. (1952). *The yearling*. New York: Harper & Row.

Taylor, M. (1981). *Let the circle be unbroken*. New York: Dial.

Taylor, M. (1976). *Roll of thunder, hear my cry*. New York: Dial.

White, E. B. (1952). *Charlotte's web*. New York: Harper & Row.

NAEYC is . . .

. . . a membership supported organization of people committed to fostering the growth and development of children from birth through age 8. Membership is open to all who share a desire to serve and act on behalf of the needs of and rights of young children.

NAEYC provides . . .

. . . educational services and resources to adults who work with and for children, including

- **Young Children,** *the* Journal for early childhood educators
- **Books, posters,** and **brochures** to expand your knowledge and commitment to young children, with topics including infants, curriculum, research, discipline, teacher education, and parent involvement
- An **Annual Conference** that brings people from all over the country to share their expertise and advocate on behalf of children and families
- **Week of the Young Child** celebrations sponsored by NAEYC Affiliate Groups across the country to call public attention to the needs and rights of children and families
- **Insurance plans** for individuals and programs
- **Public policy information** for informed advocacy efforts at all levels of government
- The **National Academy of Early Childhood Programs,** a voluntary accreditation system for high quality programs for young children
- **Child Care Information Service,** a computer-based, centralized source of information sharing, distribution, and collaboration.

For free information about membership, publications, or other NAEYC services . . .

. . . call NAEYC at 202-232-8777 or 800-424-2460 or write to NAEYC, 1834 Connecticut Ave., N.W., Washington, DC 20009-5786.

Information
About NAEYC

Elizabeth Jones holds a Ph.D. in sociology from the University of Southern California. She has taught preschool, primary, and college students. She has also written and consulted in early childhood education/human development. Dr. Jones is currently on the faculty of Pacific Oaks College in Pasadena, California.

Elizabeth Jones